Scientific Analysis of Archaeological Ceramics

A handbook of resources

Scientific Analysis of Archaeological Ceramics

A handbook of resources

Katherine Barclay

Published for English Heritage by Oxbow Books

Published by
Oxbow Books, Park End Place, Oxford, OX1 1HN

ISBN 1 84217 031 7

A CIP record for this book is available from the British Library

The cover image is a thin section from a Soundess Waster Swyncombe
taken from Maureen Mellor's *Oxfordshire Pottery,*
Oxoniensia 59, 1994, Plate 11, 3b

This book is available direct from
Oxbow Books, Park End Place, Oxford, OX1 1HN
(Phone: 01865-241249; Fax: 01865-794449)

and

The David Brown Book Company
PO Box 511, Oakville, CT 06779, USA
(Phone: 860-945-9329; Fax: 860-945-9468)

and

via our website
www.oxbowbooks.com

Printed in Great Britain by
The Information Press
Eynsham, Oxford

Contents

Acknowledgements

In preparing this booklet I have received every courtesy from many friends and colleagues and learned institutions. The project gained momentum with the help of members of the 'Implementation Committee' formed to fulfil the recommendations of the review of Medieval Ceramic Studies in England (Mellor 1994). It has been produced and published with the aid of grants from English Heritage for which I am most grateful. Staff at their Centre for Archaeology, especially Brian Attewell, Miles Hitchen and Sheila Keyte have kindly given me technical advice and help with preparation of the text. The figure is by Philip Magrath. I am indebted to David Brown of Oxbow Books, and to Julie Choppin for her skill in typesetting and her patience. Oxbow Books designed the cover. My principal debt is to Michael Hughes whose input was instrumental to my achieving the right breadth of information in the text. It has benefitted too from comment made by English Heritage's anonymous reader and by Alex Bayliss, Ian Freestone, Chris Gerrard, Clive Orton and David Williams; I thank them all but I take responsiblity for the errors and omissions that remain. I am grateful to Sarah Jennings for her continued faith in the project; she and Michael Hughes have provided great encouragement. My family have been models of patience and support and I thank them unreservedly.

In memoriam R L B and T L B

Portsmouth 1999

Who is this handbook for?

This handbook is principally for ceramic archaeologists, (for those handling or caring for collections, e.g. in field units or museums), to provide relevant background for discourse with archaeological scientists. It is intended to encourage the use of scientific services, by making information about them more widely available, by describing the range of information which might be sought by ceramic analysis, and by explaining (to the layperson) terms and methods used by scientists. The sections giving broad outline of methods of analysis include some technical material, abbreviated to salient points, but they are for guidance only, to explain how the sampled sherd will be affected. Details of technique can be followed up through the references. The handbook is NOT a *menu* from which to choose; the selection of methods of analysis should be made by the scientist and archaeologist *together* as members of the project team. The archaeologists should be clear about what questions they hope to answer, about the pottery and with it, while the scientist should recommend the best method or methods for attempting to answer those questions (see Bayley (ed.) 1998). Centres known at the date of publication to be providing a service are listed after each technique (see below p. 8 and pp. 39–41).

Key for Tables

Z – atomic number	see p. 15	high	see p. 4
M – Major	see p. 15	v. high	see p. 4
m – minor	see p. 15	fast	see p. 4
t – trace	see p. 15	average	see p. 4
ut – ultra-trace	see p. 15	slow	see p. 4
ppm – parts per million	see p. 15	quantitative	see p. 15
ppb – parts per billion	see p. 15	semi-quantitative	see p. 15
low	see p. 4	qualitative	see p. 15
moderate	see p. 4	half-life	see p. 22

Introduction

Given the enormous body of pottery recovered from the excavations of the last half-century, the focus of attention in ceramic research is increasingly turning away from duplicative amassing and reporting of material and towards synthetic work. Those responsible for archaeological ceramics need to understand the range of information which might be sought by scientific analysis, and to become familiar with terms and methods used by scientists, in order to judge whether possible applications of science are likely to be meaningful.

In the United Kingdom, analytical and dating methods have been applied to ceramics, but inconsistently across the country, which may in part reflect patchy knowledge of, and accessibility of, local expertise and services. Many new techniques have been developed in the last decade, and others have been put aside. There are specialist facilities in various centres, each offering some of the many techniques which differ in cost and complexity, and in suitability for given circumstances. Guidelines such as those produced in the 1980s by the pottery research groups, giving a concise summary of the principal applications of science at that time, are being brought up-to-date (PCRG 1997, MPRG in prep. SGRP in prep.).

Identification of the geographical source of ceramics is vital to the study of trade and exchange; a systematic approach to the characterisation and classification of their fabrics is a prerequisite. The integration and correlation of the local type series in any region require scientific support in the characterisation of the fabric types. The recommendations of the review of Medieval Ceramic Studies in England included the preparation of a handbook for the ceramic archaeologist, 'to improve scientific back-up to support type-series by including appropriate analyses' (Mellor 1994, 31) and to provide absolute dates where appropriate (ibid. 9).

General references: Taylor and Aitken 1997 (for dating), Shepard 1976 (a fundamental archaeological text on ceramic materials, manufacturing methods, ceramic description, processing and analysis), Freestone 1995 (a resume of the major petrographic techniques) Kingery (ed.) 1993 (demonstrating social and cultural applications), Blinkhorn forthcoming (a detailed analysis of a pottery type from a technological standpoint using analytical and experimental techniques), Rice 1987 and Orton *et al.* 1993 (both following on from Shepard).

Planning

The aims of a project will of course have been set at local level, and integrated into the regional and national research framework (Mellor 1994, Ch 6). The importance of considering the potential of ceramics at the earliest possible stage of planning has been stressed before (e.g. MAP2, 9–11). Standard procedures, from recovery of material to washing (N.B. avoid washing ceramics in acid to remove concretions), drying, marking, packing and recording, may all affect the subsequent analysis of sherds. The sooner potential specialists, including scientific analysts, are included in planning, the better (CBA 1990, IFA1991, 3 point 7). The value of results may otherwise be diminished, if recording is inadequate and extrapolation from the results becomes limited or impossible. Indeed, unless the right method of excavating material and collecting samples is planned for, some techniques, e.g. the analysis of residues or thermo-luminescent dating, may not be practicable.

The appropriateness of analysis and the need to avoid diminishing returns must both be prominent in the assessment of potential of analysis (MAP2 Ch 6). If assessment of material shows that analysis is unlikely to, or cannot, reach objectives, the courage is required to omit further study. Questions which can be answered only if *all* the material is *scientifically* analysed should be avoided; but rather than analysing a few samples of everything, a full answer should be sought from some selected group or groups of material.

Classification of sherds into groups is the basis for all further work on ceramics. The starting point for grouping into fabrics is usually a visual study with a hand lens or binocular microscope, at a power up to ×20, but this kind of examination, though sufficient and appropriate working practice for bulk processing, is subjective (see e.g. Orton *et al.,* 67–75 and 135–40). The proper definition of these fabrics 'by exact impersonal standards' (Shepard 1976) is essential to compatibility of results among workers and between different sites; it permits meaningful comparisons to be made between kinds of pottery and groups of pottery and increases the likelihood of correct attributions by others. It is the consensus of the profession that all processed pottery should be related to a recognised type series (e.g. Blake and Davey (eds) 1983), and that at local level, the characterisation of fabrics, and at regional level the definition of new fabrics/types/wares, need to be addressed through scientific analysis (Mellor 1984, 26; 31). Moreover, 'The importance of type-fabric/ware series cannot be overestimated as a means of reducing costs and increasing efficiency in processing and reporting' (Fulford and Huddleston 1991, 46).

Because the research team will need to use the results of any analysis to draw conclusions about the remainder of the group under study, appropriate handling of the whole assemblage is vital, and before analysis, careful sampling will be needed if the results are to be generalised. 'Unknown sampling bias is not a license [sic] to ignore statistical theory' (Cowgill 1995); a suitable, statistically valid, sampling scheme should be conducted (see below p. 3). The timing of selection of sherds for scientific analysis must not preclude their proper visual classification; for maximum benefit, the results of the two kinds of study must be fully linked (e.g. Cumberpatch 1993, Evans 1989). Much of the analytical work to date has been initiated on a site-by-site basis. Experience of specialists involved suggests that 'most useful results emerge from the examination of themes and issues that cut across site-based problems' (Fulford and Huddleston 1991, 49).

'The best starting point is the identification of a problem' (Rice 1987, 321). This may signal a particular technique that will have sampling constraints of its own; the scientist intended to carry out the analysis should be consulted. Often a programme of analysis will use several techniques (see below, p. 4).

When embarking on a programme of analysis, some of the questions to be considered are

- Must sherds be prepared or collected in any special way by the archaeologists?
- How much or how many samples will be needed, and will it/they be re-useable or returnable?
- Will taking or testing samples be destructive, or merely damaging, and if the latter, how much? Will the test analyse the bulk of the sherd, or its surface, or merely a small point?
- How long will it take from handing over the samples to the scientist to getting the results? Is there a backlog; who has priority; how likely are delays?
- Will the results be given raw or interpreted?
- What, in terms of scope, accuracy etc, are the limitations of the technique (i.e. what can't it tell us?)

Choosing Samples

It will usually be necessary to extrapolate from the results of the analysed sherds to other material. Orton (2000) and Rice (1987, 318–27) together provide full review of the considerations. Orton (pp. 27–29) analyses the process of sample surveying including the difficult problem of the relationship of the chosen samples to the target population. As many sherds as can be spared and as expense permits should be included in the programme of analysis, and they should be chosen by, or with the direct involvement of, the analyst who will carry out the scientific work. They should be typical, but at the same time cover the range of material of that class, and sherds other than plain body sherds should be considered; in residue analysis (see below pp. 34–5) for example, base sherds will not necessarily yield the most evidence (Charters *et al.* 1995). In general, sherds chosen should have no visible evidence of burial, e.g. no surface damage, and should be stratified, preferably from dateable, closed deposits. The 'bottom line' is whether a sherd or vessel may or should be damaged or even destroyed; in the latter case, some exactly similar material *must* be preserved for future comparisons and extrapolations. If samples of associated material (e.g. soil from the context) may be needed, contamination must be avoided.

Costs

The cost of a programme of analysis will vary with the methods being used, but all scientific techniques are expensive. One cannot afford (and nor would one wish) to apply them to more than a small proportion of any assemblage.

Petrology is often assumed as the first choice (see below p. 6, 9) partly because it is perceived to be cheaper. Thin-section preparation is certainly straightforward and is widely taught. It can be done with relatively modestly-priced equipment, for example by a ceramic archaeologist in the potshed, but an experienced technician with up-to-date equipment will produce better quality sections, and more rapidly, for a very modest fee (about £10 per slide in 2000). The interpretation of the section is likely, however, to require at least checking and confirmation by an experienced petrologist (which may double the cost), and for characterisation and provenance attribution, someone will have to undertake the often considerable background studies of local geology, place-names and comparative materials, tasks which are time-consuming and therefore usually costly.

However simple the problem appears, it should be discussed at the outset with an experienced scientist; there may be a technique not known to you (perhaps new), which is to them the obviously appropriate approach to provide a cost-effective solution to your problem. Negotiations should establish that the costs quoted include everything from preparation of the sample to statistical analysis of the results, and cover any repetitions of tests necessary for clarification of ambiguities.

In Tables 1–3 below, relative costs (low, moderate, high – compared with thin-section preparation) at the date of publication are given for the major analytical techniques. The approximate or relative speed of doing the test is indicated by slow/weeks, average/days or fast/same or next day.

Combining techniques

An ideal programme of analysis might use several techniques, scientific and archaeological, and some most convincing results have come about this way. When several techniques are proposed, because of its unique predictive aspect, petrological analysis would usually precede compositional analysis.

Examples of studies employing several techniques include Tite *et al.* (1990), using SEM, XRD, AAS, IRS, and petrology on refractory ceramics including crucibles, tuyères and furnace walls; Hughes (1995) differentiating between Spanish and Sardinian wares of similar decoration and fabric using petrology and NAA; Sheridan (1989), exploring pottery production in Neolithic Ireland by AAS, XRF and petrology; Courty and Roux (1995) examination of 3rd millennium technology in Syria, India and Iran, using binocular and electron microscopy and porosity studies of archaeological and laboratory ceramics; Maniatis *et al.* (1984) combined the results of OES, Mössbauer, X-Ray and petrological methods to classify amphorae; Waksman and Spicer (1997) used PIXE, NAA, petrography and geochemistry to distinguish local and imported wares in Pergamon.

In studies that use several different methods, analysis of the results will often benefit from special statistical techniques (see below 6).

Evaluation and publication of results

Through analysis we are seeking the relationship between the artisan and the artifact – where, when and how materials were changed into the ceramics whose remains we have to study (see e.g. Howard and Morris 1981, Kingery (ed.) 1993, Van der Leeuw 1994). This is not the place to discuss the cognitive and the cultural, but the results of analysis by themselves mean little; they must be put in context. A proper scientific report consists of analysis AND interpretation.

Reconciling the archaeological hypothesis with the results of analysis may point to a different direction of research and more analysis (see e.g. Echallier 1991). Subjective judgements must be avoided and the apparent precision of science approached with caution (statistical significance will not always equate with archaeological significance). Sometimes the results of scientific work may be at odds with the views of the archaeologists; provided the results are soundly based, such differences should not be suppressed but should be discussed in publication. To avoid misrepresentation, any integration and interpretation by others, of scientific results, must be made in consultation with the scientist who produced the results.

Several works of reference consider or give guidance on pertinent details of publication of scientific reports, including the place of appendices and fiche, and copyright and ownership of records, data and results (CBA 1990,1991; Day 1989; IFA1998).

Why are we doing it?

Scientific analysis of ceramics is usually done with one or more of the following aims in mind:

a) Description of fabrics by detailed examination of the composition of the clay body, usually for definition and/or comparison of proposed fabric types. Raw materials may be identified. Full characterisation of fabrics is necessary for correlation and integration of the local type series in any region. The identification of the geographical sources of ceramics is vital to study of trade and exchange; a systematic approach to characterisation and classification of fabrics is a prerequisite.

National reference collections of fabrics are in existence or being created for each archaeological era, aiming to demonstrate the variety of ceramics, with emphasis on a broad geographical spread of material from production sites or from well-dated contexts; a complementary National database of thin-sections of ceramics has been compiled (see Appendix A).

b) Characterisation of kiln sources. Applying the same standards of description to the products of known kilns is of the highest priority. From this base, the origins, range and distribution of wares, and their relationships to other wares should eventually be established. A variant of this approach is to compare vessels related by, say, stamps or potter's marks, to 'characterise' the potter's products.

c) Identification of the geological and geographical sources of raw materials, or provenance studies. Rocks are composed of minerals, which are themselves composed of chemical elements combined together. (A brief guide to some chemical terminology used when discussing elements is given under 2 below). Evidence for the sources of the raw materials in ceramics is contained in the minerals making up the fabric. Clays used to make archaeological ceramics typically have variable quantities of coarser inclusions (called *aplastic* inclusions) set in a finer-grained matrix. The composition of the clay matrix may be characteristic of its source. Inclusions are frequently natural to the clay though they may have been added deliberately by the potter as *temper*. Most commonly, inclusions are fragments of rocks and minerals, though they may be vegetable matter, chaff, shell, bone or crushed ceramic (grog). Petrological methods can explore these characteristics directly, indeed it may occasionally be possible to predict a geological source from the petrology of an archaeological sample (Freestone 1991, 1995, Peacock 1977b). Compositional methods, on the other hand, generally require statistical comparison of a set of results with potential geological raw materials or with ceramics from possible sources (e.g. kiln products). A single source may of course produce different fabrics, and conversely several workshops may share raw materials, producing surprisingly similar fabrics (for a fuller discussion of these more anthropological aspects see e.g. Arnold 1989, Peacock and Williams 1986).

d) Investigation of technology, of manufacturing techniques and use/function. How were items made; what from; were materials prepared in any way, by refining, e.g. washing, or by mixing, e.g. with temper, and why; how well were they fired; was the surface of the item changed, e.g. decorated, trimmed, slipped; what were they used for? Scientific techniques can enhance observation (e.g. radiography, optical and electron microscopy), or they may elicit physical evidence of, say, firing temperatures, or porosity (e.g. XRD, Mössbauer, XRF, SEM; see below 1.4, 1.6, 2.4, 3.2).

e) Dating. Ceramics are used more than any other artifact in evaluating the date of archaeological deposits, but generally this dating is relative, being based on the study of sequences or on association with other dated items. Scientific analysis can

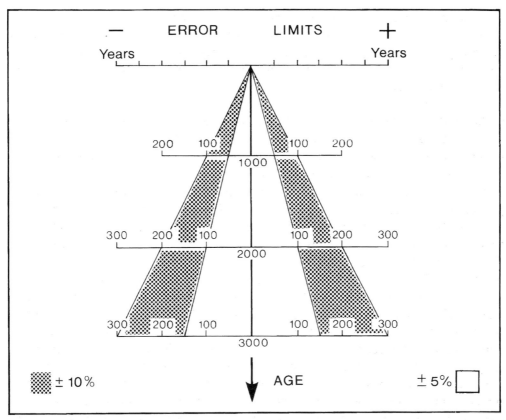

Figure 1. The effect of error limits on precision (after Bailiff 1988)

provide absolute dates, for pottery and for kilns. In the right circumstances, these dates can be measured to within a few decades, though error limits which vary considerably at different dates, are typically 5–10% (± 7% at AD 1300 = ± 35 years)

Techniques described below are grouped into these main kinds of investigation:

1 mineralogical analysis *aka* petrological, petrographic
2 compositional analysis, *aka* chemical, elemental
3 technological analysis
4 dating
5 other analyses including organic tempers and residues, fingerprints and DNA
6 statistical analysis of results is then briefly considered.
7 authentication

For each of 1, 2 and 4 there is a table summarising practical aspects of the principal techniques. Each individual technique is described in detail once, under the kind of investigation for which it is principally used; where it is also used for a different kind, cross-reference is made (e.g. organic and technological analyses both use some techniques which are described fully under compositional analysis). No technique is recommended over any other (see above p. 4, Costs). All the techniques are listed, together with alternative names and acronyms, alphabetically (see pp. 39–40).

The commentary on each technique follows a standard format, starting with description of the method (How is it done?) and its capabilities (What can it do?). Potential applications are included (When is it used?) together with a summary of recent examples; many discuss material other than British pottery. The centres known at the date of publication to be providing the technique as a service are listed by acronym (Who does it?). These are expanded in full alphabetically with addresses and contact names in Appendix B. Bibliographical references are not exhaustive; sufficient seminal works are included to cover the range of practice and application, with the bias towards readily available works on British ceramics where there was a choice. Omission is not judgmental. Articles cited are in English except when the only publication available for a particular aspect of a technique, or an especially clear application of it, is in another language. Appendices or specialist reports within excavation reports have been kept deliberately to a minimum; university dissertations and theses, and unpublished conference papers have also been avoided.

The major journals relevant to this field are: Archaeometry, Journal of Archaeological Science, Transactions of the British Ceramic Society, Journal of the American Ceramic Society, Journal of Roman Pottery Studies, Medieval Ceramics. The serials 'Art and Archaeology Technical Abstracts' and 'British and Irish Archaeological Bibliography' together provide reference to works from most countries of the world, including conference proceedings which might otherwise remain unknown.

News of scientific archaeology is available electronically; for a summary and how to gain access, see Champion 1995. The Council for British Archaeology maintains an up-to-date virtual library for UK archaeology (http://www.britarch.ac.uk/cba/info/uklinks.html). The *Science-based Archaeology Newsletter* provides news and ideas; their web-site (http://www.nerc.ac.uk/es/sbanews.htm) tells how to contact them and how to be included in the newsletter mailing.

Funding

Many learned societies, principally the Royal Archaeological Institute, the Society of Antiquaries and the British Academy, make grants, some of which are specifically for work in archaeological science, e.g. the Tony Musty Memorial Fund. The Archaeology Data Service http://ads.ahds.ac.uk and the CBA (http://www.britarch.ac.uk/cba/awards.html) give contact information.

The *Science-based Archaeology Newsletter* will describe any changes in the arrangements for research funding, which at present is awarded through the Natural Environmental Research Council, NERC.

1 Mineralogical analysis *aka* petrological, petrographic

At the least, fabrics can be described in mineralogical terms (e.g. limestone inclusions) rather than simply visually (e.g. white grits), and can be grouped like with like (Williams 1983). The identification of minerals present in pottery may point to sources of raw materials. These minerals are either residual in the clay (from the original rock or rocks) or added as temper. The identity of the minerals, their associations, their relative quantities, and characteristics of size, colour and shape, all reflect the original materials from which the clay was prepared. Combinations of these features, or more rarely, some distinctive feature, may point to possible sources that can perhaps be identified from reference material or from fieldwork. By comparison with other collections of samples in museums and research institutions (e.g. thin-sections or sherds; see below, p. 38) or by reference to geological samples and maps or texts, it may be possible to decide whether the raw materials were likely to have been available locally or must have come from outside the area, though many inclusions are too common for even this to be possible. Sometimes minerals may be sufficiently distinctive to suggest a particular geological or even geographical origin. Gerrard (1991, 190) lists some appropriate background studies (e.g. comparison with local kiln material of any period). By discriminating between fabrics, but without necessarily establishing sources, the results of petrology have nevertheless been used to construct economic models of supply and production (see e.g. Vince 1984). The principal techniques of petrological analysis are compared in Table 1.

1.1 Petrographic examination of thin sections *aka* petrological analysis, thin-section analysis, TS

How is it done? A slice of a sherd, typically 2–3 mm thick and 2cm² in area, is cut (usually through the section of the sherd, i.e. perpendicular to the surface), mounted (glued on a glass slide) and ground down until it is *c.* 0.03mm thick, gauged by characteristics of certain minerals. Simple *chemical staining* of the thin-section is sometimes used to allow distinction between rocks, which share optical properties (for example, the carbonates calcite and dolomite; Adams *et al.* 1984, after Dickson

Table 1. A comparison of the principal techniques for petrographic analysis

	THIN SECTION	TEXTURAL ANALYSIS	HMA	X-RD
Size of sample	*c.* 2sq cm	*c.* 2sq cm	20–30g	tiny 5–20mg
Damage to sherd	Yes	Yes	Yes	Slight
Will sample survive	Yes	Yes	Yes	Yes
Re-test sample	Yes	Yes	Yes	Yes
Body or surface	Both	Body	Body	Either
Parts examined	Surface paste and inclusions	Inclusions	Minerals with density >2.89	Crystalline minerals
Accuracy and	Semi-quantitative	Potentially quantitative	*c.* 250 grains to be counted for reliability	Semi-quantitative
Cost of test	£10	Moderate	Moderate	Low
Cost of interpretation	£15	Moderate	Moderate	Moderate
Speed per sample	fast/next day	average	average/days	fast/next day

1900). The sample is then examined at magnifications of up to 200 times using a petrological microscope, which allows the use of both plain and polarised light. Sherds of highly porous or friable fabric may need to be consolidated (i.e. impregnated with a bonding substance) beforehand. A polished section of a sherd may be examined by reflected light (Kingery 1974 and see below p. 20). Mineral chemistry may be examined using an analytical scanning electron microscope or electron microprobe (see below p. 21) on a *polished* thin-section (e.g. Freestone and Middleton 1987).

What can it do? Minerals in the sherd may be identified from their optical properties and the nature, size, shape, and colour of their grains in the section. Fabrics can be described and classified by these characteristics, though the terminology of description of the features seen in ceramic sections is not yet standardised among workers in ceramics (Freestone 1991, 401–2). The prepared section can be filed for reference and used repeatedly. A National database of ceramic thin-sections has been compiled (see below Appendix A). Chances of locating a source geographically are highest with coarse wares containing exotic rock and mineral fragments. The most common inclusions are quartz sands, which are rarely distinctive enough for any prediction to be made about their source from *thin-section*, (Freestone 1991, 1995, Peacock 1977b) though their associated heavy minerals may be distinctive, and textural differences may profitably be studied (see below, 1.2 Textural analysis, 1.3 Heavy mineral analysis).

It may be possible to establish if temper was added or if inclusions are natural constituents of the clay, and how the pot was formed, e.g. whether it was wheel-thrown or coil-built, and how it was decorated. The presence or absence, or the altered nature, of specific minerals may also indicate firing conditions (see below 3 Technological analysis).

When is it used? Description of fabrics; classification of fabrics; identifying raw materials; predicting sources of raw materials; matching kiln products; technological studies.

Raw materials have been identified (e.g. Shepard 1942, 1966). Fabrics have been classified (Peacock 1977a, Williams 1994). Pottery distribution patterns have been postulated (Peacock 1968) and explored (Wardle 1992, Cumberpatch 1993). Changes in sources from Roman to the Medieval in the Thames Valley have been studied (Vince 1989). Firing conditions and manufacturing techniques have also been examined (Philpotts and Wilson 1994, Shepard 1976).

Who does it? SOTN, BMAM, GLAS, CAMD, LAV, MOL, RLAHA, SASAA, SHEF, UCLR. Facilities for cutting and mounting thin sections are available in most universities (e.g. in many geology and metallurgy departments as well as archaeology).

1.2 Textural analysis *aka* grain-size analysis

How is it done? For preparation of samples, see above under petrological examination of thin sections. Essentially, this is a quantification technique; the size, shape, orientation and frequency of the grains visible in thin-section are measured and analysed. This may be done semi-automatically, with an image analyser coupled to a microscope (Whitbread 1991). The various kinds of inclusions present may be described independently or all together. Usually only a representative sample of the grains present in the thin-section is described, and the method of selection of grains affects the result (Middleton *et al.* 1985); point-counting and area counting are both used.

What can it do? Where the minerals in a ceramic are not distinctive, e.g. principally quartz as in most sandy wares, it may still be possible to use thin-sections for provenance studies as well as for description and comparison (see above 1.1).

When is it used? Description of fabrics; classification of fabrics; identifying raw materials; predicting sources of raw materials; matching kiln products. Medieval pottery kilns in West Sussex and their products have been characterised (Streeten 1980); some sources-in-common of Anglo-Saxon relief-decorated tiles have been demonstrated (Betts 1986); amphorae from Lyons have been characterised (Schmitt 1993); by comparing the smallest and largest grains in each thin-section of Torksey ware, the use over two centuries of increasingly fine quartz sand was revealed (Brooks and Mainman 1984).

Who does it? GLAS, LAV, RLAHA, SASAA, SOTN, SHEF.

1.3 Heavy mineral analysis

This technique can give useful information on such common materials as quartz sand, but rather than studying the predominant quartz, a sample is made of the tiny grains of accessory minerals. It is time-consuming. Although the evidence may be predictive, a geological source is not usually directly apparent (unlike in some thin-sections) and a larger sample is needed than for a thin-section.

How is it done? 20 to 30g of pottery are crushed and floated in a liquid with a high specific gravity (e.g. bromoform, SG 2.9; this is a dangerous chemical with strict handling protocols). The heavy minerals sink and can be separated, mounted on a slide, and identified and counted using standard petrological techniques. Some 250 grains should be studied for a reliable result. As with thin-sections, the prepared slide can be filed in a reference collection and used repeatedly.

What can it do? By comparing the heavy mineral assemblage in the sample with published geological data, it may be possible to relate the sand temper to a particular formation. The differences between samples from sherds of possibly different fabrics may be assessed, and samples from sherds may be compared with samples from possible clay or temper sources.

When is it used? Description of fabrics; classification of fabrics; predicting sources of raw materials; matching kiln products. It has been used to isolate two areas of manufacture of Romano-British black-burnished ware (Peacock 1967 and 1973, Williams 1977). It has also been applied to other Romano-British coarse wares (Wallis and Evens 1934, Williams *et al.* 1974) and post-Roman imported pottery (Peacock and Thomas 1967).

Who does it? SHEF, SOTN.

1.4 X-ray diffraction *aka* XRD

How is it done? A sample may be some individually selected inclusion or inclusions, or powdered ceramic. Some 10mg (2–20mg) of powder is used, though very small samples (µg) can be analysed by film methods. It is bombarded with X-rays which are diffracted (reflected) to produce patterns characteristic of the crystal structure of the specimen; only well-crystallised (rather than amorphous) material produces patterns. The patterns, recorded on film or chart, can be compared with standard data of known mineralogy, and quantification of mixtures may be possible with the larger samples and suitable computer facilities.

What can it do? X-ray diffraction can identify mineral phases and chemical compounds (in either clay fabrics or pigments). Powdered clay samples may produce complex diffraction patterns, but the technique is ideally suited to establishing whether or not samples are identical without having to identify all the minerals present. Alternatively, a particular kind of inclusion can be examined separately. The identification of specific (high temperature crystalline) phases in pottery can give some indication of firing temperature (Perinet 1960) or fabrication method (Philpotts and Wilson 1994); reheating of samples to create high temperature minerals has shown that identification of such minerals can sometimes indicate the composition of the original clay paste and temper (Isphording 1974).

When is it used? Description of fabrics; classification of fabrics; predicting sources of raw materials; matching kiln products. The method has been used chiefly in classifying different fabrics. For example, hard and soft-paste post-medieval porcelains have been classified on the basis of high-temperature crystalline phases (Bimson 1969); in combination with SEM and EDXA, XRD has been used further to distinguish glassy, bone-ash and soapstone and hardpaste porcelains, and to separate the products of some English factories (Tite and Bimson 1991). The technique has been successfully applied to pottery pigments (Shepard 1971, Chase 1971, Stos-Fertner *et al.* 1979). Gerard *et al.* (1997) have identified clay sources.

Who does it? BMAM, BRAD, CFA, CLRC, UCLR.

1.5 Infra-red absorption spectrometry, *aka* Fourier transform, FTIR

How is it done? A sample of 2–5 mg is used to prepare and *c.* 1mg powder is mixed into a pellet or a single inclusion may be studied. Infra-red radiation is focused on to the specimen, the molecules of which will vibrate, at frequencies characteristic of the atomic groups present. Some infra-red light will be absorbed if its frequency is the same as the vibration frequency of the specimen molecules. The extent of absorption at each wavelength is indicative of the atomic groups in the specimen (Tite 1972, 288–91, 356–8).

What can it do? It can be used to identify mineral phases and chemical compounds in clay fabrics and pigments. As it is applicable to poorly- in addition to well-crystallised minerals, it complements X-R D (see 1.4).

When is it used? Eissa *et al.* (1974) examined iron and colour in Egyptian Black Ware. Eiland and Williams (2000) found different IR spectra for different fabric types, reflecting different mineralogies and firing conditions; they refer to earlier IR papers and spectra libraries.

Who does it? CLRC, MJH, RLAHA.

1.6 Mössbauer spectroscopy *aka* nuclear gamma resonance spectroscopy

The Mössbauer effect occurs for only a few chemical elements of which, in ceramic analyses, what is usually of interest is the state of the iron, i.e. is it ferrous or ferric and is it combined in clay minerals, iron oxides or silicates.

How is it done? Gamma-ray radioactivity produced from a standard source is absorbed by matching nuclei in the sample; the extent of absorption is indicative of sample composition. By re-firing samples, and re-measuring their Mössbauer spectra to establish at what temperature they change, the ceramic's firing temperature may be determined. (See Cranshaw *et al.* 1985)

What can it do? A Mössbauer absorption spectrum gives not only elemental data but also information on the local crystallography (i.e. environment) around the iron, identifying and quantifying (relatively) various iron-bearing minerals in a sample. The oxidation state of the iron, and whether it is present as oxides or silicates or within the clay minerals, may help in determining firing temperatures.
Constraints: Post-depositional weathering and consequent changes in the oxidation state of the iron reduce precision.

When is it used? The technique has been used to define clay sources (Gangas *et al.* 1971). The analyses to estimate the firing temperature of Cheam kiln products (Cousins and Dharmawardena 1969), included an examination of the relation between oxidised iron minerals and colour. The nature of the black colour on early Cypriote and Nubian C-group black-topped pottery has been explored (Makundi *et al.*1989). Feathers *et al.* (1998) examined the evidence for the firing atmosphere of Missouri Indian pottery. Similar analyses have been applied to ancient Egyptian pottery by Eissa *et al.* (1974) and to pottery and clays from Tel Ashdod, Israel, and Eastern Cyprus (Hess and Perlman 1974).

Who does it? Now used more for technological analysis.

1.7 Other methods of examination

Raman microscopy This form of spectroscopy with a beam of one micron or 1/1000 mm, using a microscope linked to a computer, can be focused on a very small area, at up to *c.* ×500 magnification, for example upon a single grain to identify an unknown inclusion. It gives immediate results. No applications to archaeological ceramics have yet been published, but research is in progress (M Hughes, pers. comm.; Turrell and Corset 1996). *Methods discussed in Section 4.1–5* may also provide information on mineralogical composition, although they are now primarily employed to investigate firing conditions.

2 Compositional *aka* elemental, chemical, including trace element, analysis

The techniques in this section are used to determine concentrations in the ceramic of selected major, minor and trace elements, here defined respectively as more than 2%, between 2 and 0.01 and less than 0.01%. Similarities or differences in the concentrations or ratios of certain elements, (or historically their presence or absence), are compared. Results may be *quantitative* (where elements are identified and the amounts present measured), *semi-quantitative* (where relative amounts are established) or *qualitative* (where elements are identified but not amounts). Quantitative elemental data can be used for description and definition; this may require additional analyses of a comparative series of standard specimens of known composition, resembling that of pottery (known as *standards*), to calibrate scientific equipment.

Major elements usually affect the overall character of pottery and variations in composition at this level may reflect technological changes. Minor and trace element concentrations may define clay sources or kiln products and discriminate between pottery fabrics. Attempts to relate the element concentrations of fired clay products to the raw geological material have been most successful where considering widely disparate clay sources and/or ceramic traditions.

There are 92 naturally occurring elements and their concentrations in clays vary enormously; the various methods of compositional analysis can detect different subsets of them. Elements are conventionally referred to, and arranged in order by, the variable known as atomic number or Z (this is the number of protons in an atom of a particular element). Isotopes are different forms of the same element (having differing numbers of neutrons in their atoms). For any element, all isotopes have the same atomic number, but each has a different atomic weight (which is the sum of the numbers of protons and neutrons in an atom of that isotope). Among the isotopes of the element carbon, for example, are ^{12}C and ^{14}C. Both have the same atomic number, or Z, of 6 (with 6 protons per atom), though their atomic weights are 12 and 14, (for they have 6 and 8 neutrons respectively per atom).

For some techniques, the range of elements detectable is given by reference to Z. If it is not known which elements may be distinctive or discriminating, as many as 35–40 may be recorded though as few as four have been used (Tubb *et al.* 1980).

From statistical theoretical considerations, a minimum of ten has been proposed, and nowadays this minimum is exceeded comfortably by practically every application of elemental/compositional analysis to ceramics.

Compositional techniques differ in their scope; a comparison of some more widely used methods is given in Table 2. AAS has a low detection limit, and so may be preferred for very small samples. NAA detects a greater number of elements, but for some e.g. Calcium, it is less reliable. ICP has a wider range (including elements which may be crucial), than AAS, but narrower than NAA. References surveying the potential of the principal techniques include Bishop *et al.* 1982, Bennet *et al.* 1989, Hatcher *et al.* 1995, Hughes *et al.* 1991, Jones 1986, Neff (ed.) 1992.

Chemical analysis has been applied more to fine, well-mixed fabrics because experimental difficulties can arise with coarser gritted bodies, although the inclusions may be separated from the paste for analysis (Fillieres *et al.* 1984), and there are statistical techniques suited to addressing the problem of 'diluting' by

Table 2. A comparison of some widely-used techniques for compositional analysis

	AAS	ESCA	ICP-OES	NAA	X-RF
Size of sample	Powder 10mg-1g	Powder c.1mg or section	5mg-1g	Powder 20mg-1g	Surface or powder 100mg-2g
Damage to sherd	Slight	Slight	Slight	Slight	None or slight
Will sample survive	No	Yes	No	No	Yes
Re-test sample	No		No	Yes	Yes
Body or surface	Body	Surface	Body	Body	Body or surface
Parts examinable	*c.* 50 elements	*c.* 80 elements	30-40 metallic elements	*c.* 80 elements	80 elements
Sensitivity	m,t 10ppm - 100%	M,m	M,m,t 100ppm - 10%	M,m,t,ut ppb - 100%	M,m,t 50ppm - 100%
Accuracy and precision	High 2%	Semi quantitative	High 1-5%	High 1-5%	Semi quantitative
Cost of test	Low	High	Low	V. High	Low - Moderate
Cost of interpretation	Moderate	Moderate	Moderate	High	Low
Speed of sample	average /days	fast/next day	fast	slow -- half-life time	fast

temper. Topping and Mackenzie (1988) have considered the impact of organic temper on results. The preparation of clays, especially blending and purification, and the subsequent changes through firing and burial, may all have an impact on the analytical results (Kilikoglou *et al.* 1988, 37). Even in apparently straightforward circumstances, with established methods, the incorporation in analytical pro- grammes of standards is recommended, to improve the potential for comparison between different sets of published results and between different laboratories (Hatcher *et al.* 1995). The difficulties of making such comparisons are discussed by Mirti *et al.* (1995).

Any choice of technique to be used for a project will inevitably be influenced by equipment available to the chosen laboratory. For several techniques, access to a nuclear reactor, and so to a laboratory with the right equipment and facilities for handling radioactive materials, is essential. For most, a computer is required for data processing, and a statistician to interpret the experimental results. The results provided to the archaeologist are likely to be given with error terms or standard deviations rather than as absolute values.

Precision is the exactness or closeness of the result to the true figure. *Accuracy* is the repeatability or reproducibility, i.e. the closeness of a second result to the first. (It is possible to be precise but inaccurate, perhaps because of problems with an instrument; many people confuse the two terms.) *Sensitivity* has been used in two senses; firstly, for the minimum amount detectable, expressed in terms of major, minor, trace- (parts per million) or ultra-trace (parts per billion) elements; secondly, as the lowest (by atomic number) element detectable (see Bishop *et al.* 1990).

When is it used? Description of fabrics (especially of very fine paste where inclusions don't help); identifying raw materials; classification of fabrics; characterisation of kiln sources; matching kiln products.

Pitfalls of Nomenclature

Optical emission spectroscopy (OES) which was used for elemental analysis in the 1960s, 1970s and 1980s (e.g. Jones 1986) has been superseded by ICP-OES.

Until the late 1980s, investigations of ceramics by inductively-coupled plasma spectrometry (*aka* ICP or ICPS) used only the 'optical (or atomic) emission' kind, and it was sufficient to use the briefer name and acronym as here. In the early 1990s, the 'mass' kind of ICP began to be used for ceramics and in published work from about this time, there may be some ambiguity in naming and acronyms. The term 'mass spectrometry' had been widely used for what is now more correctly called thermal ionisation mass spectrometry.

OES	now obsolete
mass spectrometry	now thermal ionisation mass spectrometry
ICPS	at first only the 'OE' kind, later called

ICP-OES or ICP-AES   to distinguish it from
ICP-MS

2.1 Inductively-coupled plasma spectrometry *aka* ICP or ICPS

There are now two principal methods, ICP-OES and ICP-MS. Both give quantitative analyses for many elements in each sample. A solution is prepared from some 50mg of powdered sample and between 10 and 30 samples are needed. The dissolution of the samples is likely to take at least as long as the actual analysis. There is great potential for analysis of large numbers of samples to very low concentrations of elements.

   The use of plasma arcs (Keirs and Vickers 1977) has led to improved quantitative data. Both methods use a plasma (very high temperature) source as a means of breaking down the sample solution into its constituent atoms.

2.1.1 *Inductively-coupled plasma-optical emission spectrometry or ICP-OES* aka *ICP-AES, atomic emission spectrometry*

How is it done? At this high temperature, energy is released from the sample in the form of visible light composed of characteristic line spectra, the intensities of which are proportional to the concentrations of the elements present in the sample. The elements may be distinguished with the aid of a light dispersing system, or grating. Detection of the elements can be simultaneous (which is more expensive), or sequential, (where elements are scanned in turn, for perhaps one second each).

What can it do? Once the samples have been prepared (see above 2.1), in a day, typically, some thirty to fifty samples can each be analysed for twenty or more elements. It is possible to measure in the same solution major, minor and a selection of trace elements.

Who does it? BMIF, BRAD, CFA, GLAS, LAV, MJH, RHUL, SASAA.

When is it used? Local fine wares of Calabria from seventh to second century BC have been distinguished from Corinthian, Ionian and Attic wares and from other imitations (Mirti *et al.* 1995). Colchester 'Samian' has been investigated (Storey *et al.* 1989).

2.1.2 *Inductively-coupled plasma-mass spectrometry ICP-MS*

How is it done? There is much interest in the application of lasers to vaporise a sample in solid form, but to date, most quantitative work has involved the use of samples in solution (see above 2.1). The solution is introduced into a plasma which is connected to a mass spectrometer. The plasma breaks the sample down into charged ions of its constituent elements. These ions can be moved through the mass spectrometer to its detector, which essentially counts the atoms (hence its extreme sensitivity). By collection of these ions and measurement of their intensities, the original concentrations of different elements present in a sample can be assessed.

What can it do? It is potentially a method for providing accurate analysis simultaneously, on a very wide range of elements in a sample (a wider range of elements than ICP-OES, though not including some of the major elements). It is capable of extremely low detection limits to rival those of neutron activation analysis, which, in archaeological science, it may well in time replace. No work on archaeological ceramics has yet been published; the technique is discussed by Jarvis *et al.* (1992).

Who does it? RLAHA, SURRCA.

2.2 Thermal ionisation mass spectrometry, *aka* mass spectrometry

This technique, which has been used in archaeology for some time, is to be distinguished from ICP-MS, which has been used in archaeology only since the early 1990s.

How is it done? Solid or powdered samples of a few milligrams are vaporised in, for example, a spark discharge and, during the process, atoms present become ionised and show electrical charge characteristics. These charged particles can be made to move at high speeds and can then be separated into basic atomic groups with the aid of a strong magnetic field, and the elements present can be detected (see Tite 1972 92–4, 302–3.)

What can it do? The applications into archaeology have all been for the isotopes of lead. As the relative abundance of naturally occurring lead isotopes varies significantly between different ore sources, the source of the lead used in glazes and pigments may be identified. The same data may be used to define kiln products and describe pottery fabrics.

When is it used? There have been investigations into ancient glazes; there is a project underway at the Smithsonian Institute, Washington, on tin-glazed post-medieval pottery.

Who does it? RHUL.

2.3 Atomic absorption spectrometry, AAS

How is it done? A sample, typically 10mg–1gram, is dissolved, and vaporised by spraying into a flame (whose temperature is very much lower than a plasma as in ICP above, but still able to break up into atoms the material sprayed into it). Light characteristic of one of the elements to be analysed is shone through the sample, which absorbs the light in proportion to the concentration of that element in the vapour. The absorption is measured. Analysis of the same sample solution is repeated for each element in turn. Several elements may be analysed simultaneously using multi-element spectroscopic lamps. The technique is described by Hughes *et al.* (1976).

What can it do? The technique is extremely precise over a range from *c.* 0.0001 to 100%; it is used for analysis of major, minor and trace elements. The method of sampling is more suited to fine wares with few visible inclusions where a small sample is more likely to be representative of the body/paste/material/sherd.

When is it used? A series of analyses on pottery of wide-ranging type and date from Pella of the Decapolis has been reported (Bower *et al.* 1975) as have studies of Hellenistic and Roman fine wares (Hatcher *et al.* 1980) and Romano-British pottery (Tubb *et al.* 1980). Progress has been made in matching wares to likely kilns in north China (Pollard and Hatcher 1994).

Who does it? SURRCA.

2.4 X-ray fluorescence spectrometry *aka* XRF, including wavelength-dispersive XRF, WD-XRF and energy-dispersive, ED-XRF, (*aka* EDXA, EDAX), and the electron probe microanalyser *aka* electron microprobe, EPMA

The X-ray milliprobe is obsolete.

How is it done? A sample of surface area from 1mm to *c.* 4cm^2, or of powder 100mg–2g, is bombarded with X-rays (in XRF) or electrons (in EPMA) so that the excited atoms of the sample emit characteristic X-radiation fluorescence. The radiation from many elements in the sample can be identified, and the intensity of a particular energy or wavelength of emitted radiation is proportional to the concentration in the sample of the associated element. Results can be quantitative by comparison with standards of known composition.

There are two kinds of 'conventional' XRF:

a) *Wavelength-dispersive XRF (WD-XRF)* This is an accurate quantitative technique which can measure 15+ elements (including major, minor and trace elements) per sample. It requires pressed or fused pellets made from powdered ceramic and cannot be used directly on whole objects or sherds. This kind of equipment, which is relatively expensive, is being used still (e.g. in France by Picon and in the past at the Louvre, and in Germany by Schneider(1989)).

b) *Energy-dispersive XRF (ED-XRF)* With this method, quantitative analysis is possible given careful sample preparation and calibration using standards. Although it can be used to examine pressed pellets of powdered ceramic, for trace elements, the detection limits are considerably poorer than with WD-XRF. It can be operated either as a free-standing machine, or together with a scanning electron microscope or SEM (see below, 4.5). When a backscattered SEM image is used, the grey level of the image changes progressively with the atomic number of the elements present. Much compositional work on ceramics is now using this version, combining the amazing clarity and depth of field of the SEM with an ED-XRF detector so that a point or area of what is seen 'on screen' can be analysed. Whole objects or sherds can be looked at with either version; with the SEM version, results are likely to be semi-quantitative.

EPMA *aka* the electron probe microanalyser, electron microprobe (the X-ray milliprobe is obsolete.) With this variant of the technique, an electron beam systematically scans the sample surface so that variations in elemental concentration can be determined, or even 'mapped' (see Freestone 1982).

What can it do? The ability to analyse specific areas on a surface or very small parts of a sample is useful for examining sherd cross-sections in great detail (e.g. a fabric/ glaze or fabric/pigment interface), for identification and analysis of individual inclusions and for considering the matrix rather than the inclusions. Elements can be analysed simultaneously using semi-automated and portable equipment, which is ideal for speedy, non-destructive qualitative analyses.

When is it used? The sources of Roman samian wares from France and Italy have been differentiated (Picon *et al.* 1971, Picon *et al.* 1975, Widemann *et al.* 1975). Density measurements and EDXA have together been used to compare redwares from Delft, Meissen, Staffordshire and China (Anders *et al.* 1992). A characterisation of fifth century Mediterranean amphorae production has been proposed (Ramola *et al.* 1993). Ancient and modern Korean Celadons have been compared using EDXA results combined with SEM and macroscopic attributes (Koh Choo 1995). A broad study by Freestone and Rigby (1988), using SEM and EDXA, compared pre-Roman and Roman material, both native and imported, to explore standardisation and changing quality of pottery production. SEM and EDXA have been used to investigate glazing technology in a kiln group (Hurst and Freestone 1996).

Who does it? BMIF, BRAD, CFA, CLRC, MJH, NMS, RLAHA, UCLR.

2.5 Particle- or Proton-induced X-ray Emission analysis *aka* PIXE

How is it done? A sample of *c.* 1mg powder or a cut section is used, so there is little or no damage to the sherd in study. The sample is bombarded with a beam of protons; in other respects the technique is comparable to XRF above. The method is described by Johannson and Campbell (1988).

What can it do? PIXE has the advantage of low 'background noise' and so has much better (lower) detection limits for trace elements than XRF; it can give concentrations of major, minor and trace elements, to a reported accuracy of $\pm 5\%$. The process can be automated, and elements can be analysed simultaneously. Grime and Watt (1993) summarise recent applications.

When is it used? Papuan pottery has been analysed to trace its source (Rye and Duerden 1982). Imports into prehistoric communities have been studied (Jacobson *et al.* 1994). Pottery found in the Middle East has been identified as Chinese (Fleming and Swain 1992).

Who does it? RLAHA use a related technique, scanning PIXE.

2.6 Neutron activation analysis *aka* NAA

How is it done? Powdered samples of 10 to 100mg (typically 50mg) are, by bombardment in a nuclear reactor, transformed into radioactive isotopes of the elements in the sample which emit radiation. Each element produces a characteristic amount of isotope proportional to its concentration in the specimen being studied. The same sample will need to be analysed soon after irradiation to examine the short-lived activity, and up to several weeks later, for longer-lived activity (depending on the *half-life* of the elements, which is the time taken for their radioactivity to decline by half). Elements are identified/quantified by comparison with known standards irradiated at the same time. Twenty or more elements (of all those detectable by NAA) will be chosen for recording to suit both the project and the investigating laboratory (Jones 1986 pp18–20).

What can it do? Up to forty elements can be analysed simultaneously. Topping and Mackenzie (1988) have considered the impact of organic temper on results.

When is it used? NAA is probably the most widely used elemental technique for provenence studies. Techniques of multivariate analysis are now routinely used on neutron activation results (e.g. Stilke *et al.* 1996).

It has been used to define medieval kiln material (Aspinall 1977), and as an aid to pottery fabric definition (Hunter 1979). The Bell Beaker tradition has been critically examined (Rehman *et al.* 1989). Aspects of the Romano-British pottery industry of Crambeck (E. Yorks) have been clarified (Evans 1989). Typological versus archaeological groupings of ceramics have been compared (favourably) using NAA groupings (Mommsen *et al.* 1994, Stilke *et al.* 1996). Pottery evidence for interregional contact not detectable typologically has been revealed (Gunneweg *et al.* 1994).

Who does it? BRAD.

2.7 X-ray photoelectron spectroscopy *aka* XPS, electron spectroscopy for chemical analysis, ESCA

How is it done? A sample of *c.* 1mg powder or a cut section (*c.* 5mm × 1mm thick) is used, so there is little or no damage to the sherd in study. The technique records the Binding Energy (BE) needed to release electrons when the sample is bombarded with X-rays. Analysis can resolve the distinctive BEs of different elements. A given element is identified by characteristic BEs and quantified by the intensity of the energy peaks.

What can it do? X-ray photoelectron spectroscopy can, at or close to the surface of the sample, give concentrations of major and minor (but not trace) elements, including elements where Z<10 except hydrogen and helium. It is a semi-quantitative method. Elements can be analysed simultaneously. Variations in a stratum (e.g. a prepared broken edge or section of a sherd) may be studied while being abraded a few atomic layers at a time, to detect any change with depth in chemical composition (through a distance of – i.e. with a resolution of – one micron).

When is it used? for a study where carbon was a possible surface colourant, see Gillies and Urch (1983); oxidation states of iron in 13th-century Bahamian local ceramics have been studied (Lambert *et al.* 1990).

Who does it? CLRC.

2.8 Other techniques of chemical analysis

Auger Spectroscopy is another extremely sensitive elemental surface analysis which has been used to examine composition variation over microscopic depths which is especially suited to examining surface-to-body junctions, e.g. slip, glaze to body junctions.

   Wet chemical analysis, although lengthy and wholly unsuitable for large numbers of sherds, has in the past been effectively used on a small scale (Caley 1947, Jones 1997).

3 Technological analysis

Some techniques can be used to investigate how pottery was made and why the methods and materials used were chosen. The majority of the mineralogical techniques already considered (1.1, 1.4–.7) are relevant; for example, mineral states may be examined in thin-section; SEM, X-RD and MoSS can all reveal evidence of changes in the structure of ceramics or of minerals within; firing temperatures of pottery may be estimated by studying mineral changes or by thermal analysis. The potter's ability to control firing temperature might be interpreted as a sign of sophisticated technology; vitrification and reduced porosity suggest use with liquid perhaps as containers, (though permeability might have been desired, to cool contents of a vessel by evaporation). The classical text is Shepard 1976; Rice 1987 and Tite 1988 consider more recent developments and potential.

Other studies, often comparing original and replicate ceramics, have examined the colour, hardness, porosity or specific gravity of pottery; these are reviewed by Rice (1987 ch 11 and 12; and see also Combining techniques above, p. 4–5). The examination of the structure of a vessel may give clues to its forming, including how it was decorated. Temper was crucial to successful firing in the less controlled conditions of bonfire firings and early kilns (Woods 1986). Tensile strength and thermal shock-resistance of finished ceramics have been shown to vary with coarseness of temper, which has therefore been used to suggest whether certain types of vessels were for storage or cooking or serving (Steponaitis 1984). The change from the calcareous ceramics of Anglo-Saxon Canterbury to more evenly tempered fabrics may be related to increased firing temperatures (Mainman 1982; but see Woods 1986). The effects of quartz temper on the properties of ceramics have been explored (Kilikoglon *et al.* 1998; Vekinis and Kilikoglon 1998). By comparing the smallest and largest grains in each thin-section of Torksey-type ware, the use over two centuries of increasingly fine quartz sand was revealed (Brooks and Mainman 1984). The analysis of refractory ceramics (e.g. crucibles, tuyeres, furnace linings) provides evidence for both the metal-producing and the ceramic technologies (see e.g. Tite *et al.* 1990). Vogt *et al.* (1997) used petrography and geochemistry to reconstruct the manufacturing process of tiles from Constantinople. Tite (1992) describes the growing role of the SEM in explaining technological choices, by the assessment of physical properties of raw materials and finished ceramics.

Classifications of kilns have been proposed which include discussion of their technology (for medieval pottery, see Musty 1974; for Romano-British pottery, see Swan 1984). *Experimental kiln firings* are undertaken both to explore kiln technology and in conjunction with the laboratory examination of ceramics (see below 3.4). MoSS (1.6) has been used in a firing study of the terracotta statues of horses and warriors of the Qin dynasty (221 BC) in China (Qin Guangyong *et al.* 1989). The firing temperature of a kiln has been estimated from the composition of contained slaggy material using XRD and IRS (1.4–5; Shoval 1993).

3.1 Thermal analysis

Several methods have in the past been used to explore changes in pottery during heating – *differential thermal analysis* (how a pottery sample changes temperature); *thermogravimetric analysis* (how the sample's weight changes); and *thermal expansion measurements* (what expansion and shrinking occur). By comparison with standards these changes may be interpreted, usually in terms of 'equivalent firing temperature' rather than attempting to determine exact original firing temperatures. The techniques are more reliable below 600 and above 900°C, and their accuracy is poor, being about ±30 to 100°C. (See e.g. Tite 1972, 297–8)

Pore structure is dependent on the type of clay employed and on firing. For higher-fired wares, observations of pore size and structure and measurement of porosity before and after refiring, can be used to estimate firing temperatures. Shoval *et al.* (1991; 1993) have investigated the behaviour of raw materials including temper, to suggest some have technological advantages. Collins (pers. comm, at NRG) is using mercury intrusion porosimetry.

3.2 Electron microscopy including transmission electron microscopy, TEM, and scanning electron microscopy, SEM

For the examination of pottery, the use of the transmission electron microscope or TEM, which involves replicas or thin sections and is more time-consuming and expensive, is less common than the scanning electron microscope or SEM, which requires only a fresh fractured surface (though this must be coated with gold or carbon). Freestone and Middleton (1987) describe applications to ceramic analysis, and Tite (1992) reviews potential.

How is it done? A high energy electron beam is passed through a series of magnetic lenses that focus the beam to light a minute area of the pottery sample. The pattern of electrons which bounce off the specimen is either recorded on a fluorescent screen (transmission electron microscope, TEM), or converted to a television image (scanning electron microscope, SEM). In SEM, the electron beam can be moved across the sample (hence scanning). The amount of magnification (up to ×100,000) is the ratio of the size of the image on the screen to the size of the area being examined on the sample. The results can be photographed.

Either method can be used in conjunction with some other analyses; for example, ED-XRF (see above 2.4) can be used to identify elements present in small areas of the sample.

What can it do? Information on the surface topography and structure can be obtained, and the structure and state of clay particles in the matrix can be examined to establish details of, say, firing conditions and procedures and manufacturing techniques including details of slip, paint and/or glaze layers. Physical properties of raw materials – plasticity, dry shrinkage, green strength – or of finished ceramics – permeability, strenth, thermal shock resistance – may be assessable (Tite 1992). If a backscattered SEM image is used, the image shows the presence of lighter and heavier elements (by atomic number) in terms of grey level; it may be possible to quantify some aspects – firing temperature for example. The TEM has the greater resolution and capacity for crystallographic identification.

When is it used? Examination by TEM of replicas of Greek black- and red-figured pottery and Roman samian ware clarified understanding of the use of slips and of the atmospheric conditions during firing (Hofmann 1962). The lustre decoration of some 13th century Islamic wares has been explored by TEM (Kingery and Vandiver 1986). The scanning microscope has been used to examine the structural changes that occur in clay as it is fired and to estimate firing temperatures (Freeman and Rayment 1968, Maniatis and Tite 1981); the vitrification and porosity of a group of calcareous Near Eastern pottery have been compared to differentiate firing temperatures (Tite and Maniatis 1975). Analysis of haematite-coated wares of the early Iron Age has shown that while some do bear applied crushed haematite, others were burnished or have ferruginous clay slip (Middleton 1987). Technological reasons for some features of Iznik pottery have been explored (Tite 1989). Courty and Roux (1995) looked at evidence of throwing method. A broad study by Freestone and Rigby (1988) using SEM and EDXA (syn. ED-XRF, 2.4), compared pre-Roman and Roman material, both native and imported, to explore standardisation and changing quality of pottery production (See also Rigby *et al.* 1989).

Who does it? BRAD, BMIF, CFA, NMS, RLAH, SASAA.

3.3 X-ray and Xeroradiography

How is it done? X-rays penetrate more deeply into or through less dense materials, and the relative penetration can be recorded on a suitable medium. In X-ray radiography, this is film, while in Xeroradiography a latent image is captured on a special plate (electrically charged, selenium-coated) and transferred to paper using toner (as in photocopying, hence 'xero'). Lang and Middleton (1997) review methodology and applications including a chapter (3) devoted to ceramics. Direct digital radiography, computed tomography and high-resolution microfocus X-ray tubes are all innovations predicted by Middleton to be employed in ceramic analysis. Digital image processing can be used in interpreting images (Higgins 1997 provides a clear explanation).

What can it do? Radiography can show clay-forming techniques and give information about inclusions, and being non-destructive, may be suitable for rapid survey of pottery fabrics or to complement petrography. Xeroradiography, by its property of enhancing discontinuities, can be used to examine joins and the orientation of voids or inclusions, to determine forming techniques. It shows much finer details in ceramics than conventional X-rays; it is particularly suitable for less dense materials. If it is likely that TL (see below 4.2) might be used to date a ceramic artifact, this should be done first, or samples taken, because X-rays may alter the result.

When is it used? X-radiography has been used to study clay forming techniques (Rye 1977) and to show that the black surface colouring on some ceramics produced in reducing conditions may be the result of intense absorption of light by iron (Fe) and titanium (Ti4+) ions (Manning 1975). Xeroradiography has been used (despite the complication of X-ray absorption by lead glaze) to show that a medieval aquamanile was coil-built (Nenk and Walker 1991, fig 2), and to illustrate and interpret features of a medieval jug (Tite 1988, fig 1a and b).

Carr (1993) identified within a fabric group, sherds likely to have belonged to the same vessel. Middleton (1995) explored evidence for change in paste texture in parallel with change from hand building to wheel throwing. Vandiver (1988) identified surface modification by paddle-and-anvil of a Neolithic storage vessel from China.

Who does it? BM, OAL.

3.4 Experimental firings, including kiln firings

What can it do? The construction, firing and monitoring of experimental kilns and ceramics based on excavated evidence can provide insights into the technology and economics of pottery manufacture. Results appeared in the 1980's in the *Bulletin of the Experimental Pottery Firing Group*.

When is it done? In their comprehensive review of one ceramic industry, Coleman-Smith and Pearson (1988) included the results of experimental reconstructions and firings of kilns. Woods (1989) presents the results of a decade of experiments with open bonfire firings, while the Bickley Ceramics project continues to investigate the firings of simple kilns and reproduction ceramics (see e.g. Dawson and Kent 1999). MacDonald (1988) has made replica medieval jugs and attempted to reproduce glazes. Newell (1995) has followed medieval recipes to explore glaze formation. A replica 'medieval-tile' making project provided valuable evidence about practicalities and economics (Hudson 1989). A likely reason for mixing shell-tempered clay with sea (rather than fresh) water – to avoid disintegration during slaking – has been demonstrated (Rye 1976). Colour co-ordinates on pottery samples fired and re-fired between 600 and 1100°C have been used to evaluate firing temperatures of archaeological samples (Mirti 1998).

Who does it? BCP, GLAS.

4   Dating ceramics

There are now three methods of dating ceramics scientifically, by looking at thermoremanent magnetism or at luminescence, usually thermoluminescence, or by radiocarbon dating of residues or temper. A comparison of the principal techniques is given in Table 3. Textbooks describing dating methods are Aitken (1990) and Taylor and Aitken (1997). English Heritage's dating service in the Centre for Archaeology, provides advice on all aspects of scientific dating, and can help with statistical analysis, calibration and publication of results.

Table 3. A comparison of the principal techniques for dating ceramics

	RADIOCARBON DATING	LUMINESCENCE METHODS	DIRECTIONAL TRM	INTENSITY TRM
Size of sherd	Organic inclusions or residues	c.50mm x 6mm	In situ fired clay eg. kiln or hearth	As sample
Size of sample	A few grams	c.25mm x 6mm	10cm	c.5cc
Damage to sherd	Sample removal	Crushed	Sample removal	Heating
Will sample survive	No	No	Yes	Yes
Re-test sample	No	No	No	No
Preferred number of repetitions	Several	2 per artifact plus context sample	Several	Several
Precision	± 1%	± 5-15%	variable	± 5-15%
Cost of test	Moderate	High	High	Low
Cost of interpretation	Low	Moderate	Low	Low
Speed per sample	Slow/weeks	Slow/weeks	Average/days	Fast/next day

4.1 Radiocarbon dating *aka* carbon, ¹⁴C dating

Plants (and so, indirectly, animals) absorb carbon, in carbon dioxide from the atmosphere, during photosynthesis; no more carbon is absorbed after death. Some of the carbon is the unstable isotope (see above, p.15) known as radiocarbon, Carbon 14, which spontaneously decays at predictable rates, emitting particles which can be counted. The date of death can be calculated, by comparing the quantity of radiocarbon left in the artifact, or usually a sample, with a standard. Orton (1980, 90–97) gives an accessible explanation of the interpretation of results.

How is it done? Following recent refinements in technique radiocarbon dating is now possible with as little as a few grams of material (Hedges *et al.* 1992). Organic residues, such as charred deposits or lipids extracted from the ceramic, or single pieces of organic temper may be dated. The method of dating bulk material has been applied to ceramics with a high organic content, where a relatively large sample (*c.* 1kg with organic content >1%) is crushed. There are several possible sources of error, e.g. weathering, organic matter in the original clay deposit (Johnson *et al.* 1988) and so this has not been the method of choice (but see Delque Koliç 1995).

When is it used? Glover (1990, 155) analysed rice husks used to temper Thai pots, to date them. Eglington *et al.* (1997) have used extracted lipid residues for dating.

Who does it? BM, NERC, ORAU, SURRCC.

4.2 Luminescent dating, including Thermoluminescence *aka* TL dating, and Optically stimulated luminescent dating *aka* OSL, photo-stimulated, PSL, green-light stimulated, GSL, Infra-red stimulated, IRSL

Some mineral grains in clay contain radioactive elements that spontaneously decay to give a virtually constant emission of high energy radiation, but some of this electron energy becomes permanently trapped in the crystal lattice of the minerals present in the clay. When a raw clay is fired it is released as visible light, and from the time of firing new energy will be stored. The amount of stored energy since last firing can be measured as the visible light, or luminescence, emitted during testing. To stimulate the emission of the stored energy, in thermoluminescence the pottery is reheated to about 400°C, while in OSL dating it is exposed to light.

The surrounding environment also makes a steady contribution (by 'background' decay) to the ceramic's radioactive energy, known as the environmental dose. If this dose received by a sherd per year and the luminescence this induces are also measured, the age of the sherd can be calculated. Determination of the annual radiation dose requires measurements for both the sherd and the soil in which it was buried.

How is it done? Each sample requires a sherd of at least 10gm and *c.* 6mm thick, though for authenticity measurements (see below 7) as little as 3–4cu mm have been used. For the inclusion methods, 50–100mg of mineral inclusions (usually quartz) of a specific size are separated out from a crushed sherd using a magnetic separator and acid treatments. Further samples are required, to establish the annual environmental radiation dose from *c.* 1kg of the burial material, and for measuring the sensitivity of the ceramic to a known radiation dose. Site radioactivity monitoring for up to one year is also recommended.

4.2.1 *Thermoluminescence* aka *TL dating*

The thermoluminescence emitted by the ceramic is measured in two controlled heating operations. Sometimes the emission spectra are recorded, improving the accuracy of the result. There are several techniques (Aitken 1989); one, the pre-dose technique for quartz, is especially useful for porcelain and quartz-bearing ceramics less than *c.* 1000 years old.

4.2.2 *Optically stimulated luminescent dating* aka *OSL, photon-stimulated, PSL, green-light stimulated, GSL, Infra-red stimulated, IRSL*

In these methods, after inclusions, usually quartz, feldspar or zircon, are separated from a crushed sherd, their luminescence is stimulated by direct action of light. Exposure releases the luminescence very rapidly, in a matter of minutes rather than the hours necessary with TL. Rigorous precautions against accidental exposure to light have to be taken when collecting samples or separating inclusions for testing.

What can it do? The usefulness of luminescent dating for ceramics is limited by the precision of measurement which can be achieved. Under the most favourable circumstances an experimental error of ± 5% (± 35 years for thirteenth-century pottery) can be expected. Stringent on-site requirements may also be prohibitive, especially in rescue excavation. In these circumstances, an environmental dose would have to be assumed, and error allowance increased accordingly. Ideally, sherds should have been buried to a depth of at least 30cm in a homogeneous, undisturbed layer. Both the sherd and the context in which the sherd lay should be examined, so the dating specialist must be involved during or preferably before the excavation. The firing conditions of the sherd, the type of mineral examined, impurities in crystals and the nature of the burial context (especially waterlogging), all vary so much that it may not always be possible to establish a reliable date, or even to predict likely success.

When is it used? Pottery of possible Iron Age or Saxon date has been successfully attributed to the Iron Age (Zimmerman and Huxtable 1969). Medieval Sri Lankan brick samples have been dated (Clark and Templar 1988). The technique has proved valuable in authenticity testing (Fleming 1975, and see below 7). Summaries of developments in thermoluminescent dating are given by Shepherd (1997).

Who does it? DUR, NOTND, RLAHA, SURRCT, SUSX.

4.3 Thermoremanent magnetic dating *aka* archaeomagnetic dating, magnetic dating, TRM

The direction and intensity of the Earth's magnetic field vary with time and place. When clay is fired above approximately 700°C and allowed to cool, the iron oxide particles in the clay take on a new, permanent, (thermoremanent) magnetism that is parallel to, and proportional in strength to, the Earth's magnetic field in that particular region at the time of firing (Tarling 1983; see also Clark *et al.* 1988). Studies of datable samples, both geological and of fired clay have led to the establishment of regional reference curves with which samples of unknown date can be compared. Directional measurements for kilns of the Roman period onwards within *c.* 400km of Oxford produced a reference curve, although the medieval curve crosses over/loops back, reducing the chance of a reliable date. Further reference material for pre-1500 AD is still required.

How is it done? For directional measurements, in situ samples of *c.* 1000cu mm are marked with their orientation using a gyro-theodolite, before removal for measurement in a spinning magnetometer. Intensity measurements require an estimate of the orientation during the original firing.

What can it do? Directional measurements are averaged from several samples, and so need preferably a few square metres of fired clay, which has not been moved since it was last fired, though as little as half a square metre will usually be enough. This effectively restricts application to dating kilns, ovens and hearths. Intensity measurements can be made on sherds, but the variation in intensity of the Earth's magnetic field, being slower than directional variation, is of greater standard error and so less precise for dating. Less well-known uses include 'sourcing' of artifacts and technological studies (Tarling 1991).

When is it used? Intensity measurements have provided information on the variation of the Earth's magnetic field in Europe back to 7000 B.C. (Bucha 1967). An oven excavated in Waltham Abbey was dated to the first half of the thirteenth century, consistent with other evidence from the site (Clark 1993). There are many examples of kilns and ovens being dated (e.g. Rudling 1984–5, Reinders *et al.* 1999).

Who does it? GQA, PLYM.

5   Other analyses including organic tempers and residues, fingerprints and DNA

5.1 Organic residue analysis

In the right circumstances, a *residue* may survive as evidence of contents held by vessels, for storage or during preparation, e.g. cooking. The range of matter that has been identified includes salts, resins, carbohydrates, pollens, seeds, phosphates (signifying organic matter, but see Freestone *et al.* 1994) and most often oils and fats. From the residue, suggestions may be made about the use to which a vessel has been put.

How is it done? Different substances will be revealed by different methods of analysis, which include FTIR and ICP-MS (see above, 1.5, 2.1.2) sometimes with Chromatography. Immunoassay methods are now being applied (Craig and Collins 2000).

Careful choice of sherds for sampling is needed; Charters *et al.* (1995, 1997) for example, found different levels of different residues in rim sherds and base sherds. To clarify whether substances identified derive from the vessel, or rather from its burial environment, several tests may be needed, along 'concentration gradients', from mouth to base, say, or from within to outside a vessel. Ideally the programme of analysis will include tests of samples of context as well.

Chromatography: substances in solution vary in the rate at which they move or percolate through an absorbant substance, where they settle. With appropriate solvents and absorbants, the constituents of a mixed solution may be separated; what substances are present and in what proportions may then be identified. Gas chromatography uses a *c.* 3–5mg sample.

What can it do? Evans (1991) summarised the potential of these methods. Substances may be identified, but caution is required in deducing their origin (Moorhouse 1986, 109). Oil residues found on the inside of a pot may for example be from something cooked or contained in it or from proving it before use. Heron and Evershed (1993) discuss the potential for inference. Dairying, tanning, dyeing, salt and tar preparation, as well as cooking and food storage, have all been identified.

When is it used? Gas chromatography combined with thermal ionisation mass spectrometry (see above, 2.2) has been used successfully in the identification of substances in the porous walls of amphorae (Condamin *et al.* 1976, Heron and Pollard 1987), and of lipids and waxes in medieval cooking-pots (Charters *et al.* 1995). Nuclear magnetic resonance combined with isotopic analyses using mass spectrometry identified different groups of residues in round and flat pots that suggested they had had different uses (Sherriff *et al.* 1995).

Who does it? BRAD, BRIS, CAMD, GLAS, LONE, NRG, SASAA.

5.2 Organic temper analyses

Shell, bone, dung and vegetable matter have all been identified as temper in ceramics; they may provide environmental evidence.

How is it done? Several techniques including those used in residue analysis have been used. Inclusions may have to be separated from the matrix by crushing, or casts may be made of impressions remaining in the sherd (see e.g. van der Veen 1993).

What can it do? Identification of botanical inclusions such as seeds and pollen may indicate local vegetation at the clay or temper source for the time of production of the ceramic. Knowledge of the effects of different types of temper may explain characteristics, including technological aspects, of vessels of certain type (see e.g. Rye 1976).

When is it used? Oxidation and chromatographic analyses have been used to establish carbon content of organic tempering materials (Kingery 1974). London (1981) investigated dung-tempered clay. Casts of impressions of plant temper have been studied (Stemler 1990). Murphy (1985) identified local vegetation from temper in pottery. Pollen and phytoliths found in residues have also been analysed (Jones 1993). (See also Glover 1990, 155, who dated rice husks used as temper by radiocarbon dating).

Who does it? BRIS, LEICS, LONE.

5.3 Fingerprints and DNA

The possibility of deducing population information about potters from fingerprints left directly upon ceramics is being explored – the genetics of fingerprints is well understood. One study in progress is considering the gender and age group of potters from their prints (Baart 1994, fn 1); another proposal would attempt to establish family groups or even sizes of workforces (Lima-de-Faria 1995). The likelihood of residual human DNA having survived firing and burial, let alone of its being unequivocally attributable to the potter, is considered remote (Heron, pers comm.; Newman *et al.* 1996).

6 Statistical analysis of results

Almost invariably the amassed results from a set of samples (for sampling, see Choosing Samples above p. 3) will have to be compared with other results, sometimes from different techniques of analysis and sometimes from different labs, or both. This will often involve complex statistics, computers and debate. Several kinds of statistical technique may need to be applied to the same data, in case apparent features of the data are more a result of the statistical method used.

How is it done? Descriptions of some of the techniques are given by Orton (1980; 1999) and Shennan (1997); those in vogue include principal components analysis (PCA), cluster analysis, discriminant analysis and consensus analysis (McMorris 1990). Details are continually being revised and many relevant papers are published in the *Computer Applications in Archaeology* series. Baxter (1988; 1992; 1994) considers refinements to different statistical techniques; Feiller and Nicholson (1991) consider modelling to review data (from grain-size analysis; see above, Textural analysis, 1.2).

What can it do? Compare sets of data from different analyses; suggest groupings of samples; allow integration of scientific results with archaeological typological data; aid interpretation of results; display scientific results in 'user-friendly' form; test hypotheses.

When is it used? The data produced from many of the methods of analysis above will have required statistical interpretation (see e.g. NAA, Hughes 1992, 159–160, fig. 2; Baxter and Beardan 1995). Examples of combining results of different sorts include: typological information with results of *thin-section analysis* (Cumberpatch 1993), *chemical* and stylistic information (Jacobson *et al.* 1994).

Who does it? AML, MJH, NOTU, UCLS; many other organisations will have facilities and staff with the necessary expertise.

7 Authentication *aka* authenticity testing

Verification of date and provenance may sometimes be necessary to confirm authenticity. Dating is more likely to be crucial, now that the sophistication of forgery includes materials indistinguishable in any other respect from the original. *TL dating* by the inclusion method (4.2.1) has been in use here for some time (Aitken 1990); even if it produces too wide a spread of values to establish a certain date, it should be accurate enough to establish antiquity.

Radiography can reveal *restoration*; La Niece (1997) gives a full description of its potential in authentication. If it is proposed to X-ray the vessel, this would affect the TL result and samples should be taken before radiography, or dating done first.

The most suitable techniques for provenance work are likely to be minimally-damaging methods which either need no more than to look at a clean surface, e.g. EPMA (see 2.4 above), Raman (1.7), or which can use very small samples, e.g. AAS (2.3).

Who does it? OAL, RLAHA.

8 Conclusion

Since this handbook was started more than five years ago, each year papers on research into applications to ceramics of scientific analysis have continued to be published, though there have been fewer practical applications appearing, and only a very few developed synthetic works. 'Serious scientific work in archaeology needs... to make progress beyond the trivial level of applying analytical techniques' (Pollard 1995, 246). The balance of funding seems still, especially in the private sector, to be weighted towards recovery and cataloguing of material and data at the expense of analysis and interpretation, a balance which this handbook may help to remedy.

In the U.K., the English Heritage advisors (see AML and CFA) will direct enquirers to appropriate scientific services. Proposals for analysis should be based on the material itself, its problems and potential, and not on what was always done in the past (Orton 2001). Once a question has been defined, whether and which scientific techniques can help answer it, and what samples are needed, can be considered. Early pilot studies may permit better structuring of projects, which are likely to be more cost-effective, and effective, as a result. Most importantly, in any ceramic study which might involve scientific analysis, experienced analysts should be included in the project planning stage; they will be able to give the best advice if fully involved at the start.

'Science is organised knowledge' Spencer 1862

Appendix A: Reference Collections

The Prehistoric Ceramic Research Group is compiling a record of collections of pre-Roman ceramics as a first step (Morris and Woodward forthcoming).

The National Roman fabric collection is held at the Department of Prehistoric and Roman Antiquities of the British Museum (Tomber and Dore 1998).

For the Early Saxon period, to c.700 A.D., there is at present no formal national collection, nor a policy for fabric samples. The Department of Medieval and Later Antiquities of the British Museum holds the most comprehensive collection of ceramics of this period, comprised principally of material from burial contexts with, increasingly, acquisitions of domestic material.

For the period from the middle Saxon to the end of medieval, the National collection, held also at the Department of Medieval and Later Antiquities of the British Museum, has been growing since 1964 (Bruce-Mitford 1964, Cherry 1986). The National Post-medieval reference collection has developed since the late 1960s and is kept by the City Museum and Art Gallery, Stoke-on-Trent (Post-medieval Archaeology 1968).

These collections held in England are complemented by collections held in the Royal Museum of Scotland (Barker *et al.* 1989), at the Department of Archaeology of the National Museum of Wales (Redknap 1988) and at the National Museum of Ireland and at the Ulster Museum.

Thin sections

A national database of ceramic thin sections, recording sections made before 1995, from prehistoric to post-medieval sherds, was compiled, co-ordinated by City of Lincoln Archaeology Unit (Vince (ed.) forthcoming). The Ceramic Petrology Group will advise of proposals to update the database (www.ceramicpetrology.uklinux.net). The data held will include a summary of the main inclusions in a section, and give its ware, vessel class, date, site, location and arrangements for access. Enquirers seeking possible comparative or reference material will be able to search the database by, say, geographical area, at local, regional or national level. The thin sections are not themselves centralised in Lincoln, but will remain at Units and laboratories throughout the U.K. The largest collections are at Southampton and the British Museum.

Appendix B: Centres undertaking analysis alphabetically by acronym

Please Note: Inclusion in this list is no commitment to provide help

AML
Scientific Dating Coordinator
Centre for Archaeology
English Heritage
23 Saville Row
London
W1X 1AB
Ms Alex Bayliss
Mr Paul Linford

BCP
Bickley Ceramics Project
c/o Somerset County Museums Service
Castle Green
Taunton
TA1 4AA
Dr D P Dawson

BMAM
British Museum
Dept of Scientific Research
London
WC1B 3DG
Dr Andrew Middleton

BMIF
British Museum
Dept of Scientific Research
London
WC1B 3DG
Dr Ian Freestone

BRAD
Department of Archaeological Science
University of Bradford
Bradford
BD7 1DP
Dr C Heron
Prof A M Pollard

BRIS
School of Chemistry
University of Bristol
Cantock's Close
Bristol
BS8 1TS
Prof Evershed

CAMD
Macdonald Institute
University of Cambridge
Downing St
Cambridge
CB2 3DZ
Dr Laurence Smith

CAMJ
Macdonald Institute
University of Cambridge
Downing St
Cambridge
CB2 3DZ
Dr Andrew Jones

CFA
Centre for Archaeology
English Heritage
Fort Cumberland
Portsmouth
PO4 9LD
Miss J Bayley

CLRC
Daresbury Laboratory
Warrington
Cheshire
WA4 4AD
Dr E Pantos

DUR
Department of Archaeology
University of Durham
Science 2, Woodside Building
Science Lab
South Rd
Durham
DH1 3LE
Dr I Bailiff

GLAS
Department of Archaeology
University of Glasgow
10 The Square
Glasgow
G12 8QQ
Dr R E Jones

GQ
GeoQuest
The Old Vicarage
Castleside
Consett
DH8 9AP
Dr Mark Noel

LAV
Archaeological Consultancy
25 West Parade
Lincoln
LN1 1NW
Dr A Vince

LONE
Department of Archaeology
University of East London
Romford Rd
Stratford
London
E15 4LZ
Dr John Evans

MJH
Dr M J Hughes
Archaeologist Scientist
4 Welbeck Rise
Harpenden
Hertfordshire
AL5 1SL
and Hon Research Fellow
Dept of History
Royal Holloway
University of London (see RHUL)

MOL
Museum of London
Specialist Services
46 Eagle Wharf Rd
London
N1 7ED
Miss P Bradley

NERC
NERC Radiocarbon Laboratory
Scottish Enterprise Technology Park
East Kilbride
Glasgow
G75 0QU
Prof A E Fallick

NMSA
Conservation and Research Lab
National Museum of Scotland
Chamber St
Edinburgh
EH1 1JF
Dr Katherine Eremin

NMSR
Conservation and Research Lab
National Museum of Scotland
Chamber St
Edinburgh EH1 1JF
Dr Anita Quye

NOTND
Quaternary TL Surveys
19 Leonard Ave
Nottingham
NG5 2 LW
Dr N Debenham

NOTU
Dept of Maths, Stats and Operational Research
Nottingham Trent University
Clifton Lane
Nottingham
NG11 8NS
Dr Mike Baxter

NRG
Postgraduate Institute of Fossil Fuels and Geochemistry
Newcastle upon Tyne
NE1 7RU
Dr M Collins

OAL
Oxford Authentications Ltd
Bolton Buildings
Grove Technology Park
Wantage
OX12 9FA
Dr Doreen Stoneham

ORAU
Oxford Radiocarbon Accelerator Unit
RLAHA
University of Oxford
6 Keble Rd
Oxford
OX1 3QJ
Dr P Pettitt

PLYM
Department of Geological Sciences
University of Plymouth
Plymouth
Devon
PL4 8AA
Prof D F Tarling

RHUL
Department of Geology
Royal Holloway University of London
Egham
Surrey
TW20 0EX
Dr N Walsh

RLAHA
Research Lab for Archaeology and the History of Art
University of Oxford
6 Keble Rd
Oxford
OX1 3QJ
Prof M S Tite

SASAA
Scottish Analytical Services for Art and Archaeology
26 Kingsborough Gardens
Glasgow
G12 9NJ
Dr E Photos Jones

SHEF
Department of Prehistory and Archaeology
University of Sheffield
Sheffield
S10 2TN
Dr P Day

SOTN
Department of Archaeology
University of Southampton
Southampton
SO9 5NH
Dr D Williams

SURRCA
Scottish Universities Research and Reactor Centre
Scottish Enterprise Technology Park
East Kilbride
Glasgow
G75 0QU
Dr R Ellam

SURRCC
Radiocarbon Dating Laboratory
Scottish Universities Research and Reactor Centre
Scottish Enterprise Technology Park
East Kilbride
Glasgow
G75 0QU
Dr G Cook

SURRCT
Scottish Universities Research and Reactor Centre
Scottish Enterprise Technology Park
East Kilbride
Glasgow
G75 0QU
Dr D Sanderson

SUSX
Department of Experimental Physics in Engineering
University of Sussex
Falmer
Brighton
BN1 9QH
Prof P D Townsend

UCLR
Institute of Archaeology
University College London
31–4 Gordon Square
London
WC1H 0PY
Prof T Rehren

UCLS
Institute of Archaeology
University College London
31–4 Gordon Square
London
WC1H 0PY
Dr C R Orton

Bibliography

Adams, A E, MacKenzie, W S and Guilford, C, 1984: *Atlas of sedimentary rocks under the microscope,* Longman Scientific and Technical.

Aitken, M J, 1989: 'Luminescence dating; a guide for non-specialists' *Archaeometry,* 31, 147–59.

Aitken, M J, 1990: *Science-based dating in Archaeology,* Longman.

Anders, G J P A, Jorg, C J A, Stern, W B and Anders-Bucher, N, 1992: 'On some physical characteristics of Chinese and European Red Wares', *Archaeometry,* 34(1), 43–52.

Andrews, G, 1991: *Management of Archaeological Projects,* English Heritage.

Arnold, D E, 1985: *Ceramic theory and cultural process,* Cambridge University Press.

Aspinall, A, 1977: 'Neutron activation analysis of medieval ceramics', *Medieval Ceramics,* 1, 5.

Baart, J, 1994: 'Dutch Redwares' *Medieval Ceramics,* 18, 19–27.

Bailiff, I K, 1988: 'The Durham TL Dating Service' in E A Slater and J O Tate (eds) *Science and Archaeology, Glasgow 1987,* BAR British series 196, 613–18.

Barker, D, Nenk, B and Redknap, M, 1989: 'The National Reference Collections of Medieval and Later Pottery' *Medieval Ceramics,* 13, 9–11.

Baxter, M J, 1988: 'A method for grouping pottery by chemical composition – a new similarity method', *Archaeometry,* 30(1), 47–57.

Baxter, M J, 1992: 'Statistical analysis of chemical compositional data and the comparison of analyses', *Archaeometry,* 34(2), 267–77.

Baxter, M, 1994: *Exploratory Multivariate Statistics in Archaeology,* Edinburgh University Press.

Baxter, M J and Beardan, C C, 1995: 'Graphical presentation of results of principal components analysis' in Huggett J and Ryan N *Computer Applications and Quantitative Methods in Archaeology 1994* BAR International series 600, 63–7.

Bayley, J, (ed) 1998: *Science in Archaeology an agenda,* English Heritage.

Bennett, WJ, Blakeley, J A, Brinkmann, R and Vitaliano, C J, 1989: 'The Provenience postulate: Thoughts on the use of physical and chemical data in the study of ceramic materials' in Blakeley and Bennett 1989.

Betts, I M, 1986: 'Analytical Analysis (sic) and Manufacturing Techniques of Anglo-Saxon Tiles' *Medieval Ceramics,* 10, 37–42.

Bimsom, M, 1969: 'The examination of ceramics by X-ray powder diffraction', *Stud Conserv,* 14, 85–9.

Bishay, A, (ed) 1974: *Recent advances in science and technology of materials* 3, Plenum.

Bishop, R L, Canouts, V, Crown, P L and De Atley, S P, 1990: 'Sensitivity, precision and accuracy; their roles in ceramic compositional databases' *American Antiquity,* 55(3), 537–46.

Bishop, R L, Rands, R L and Holley, G R, 1982: 'Ceramic compositional analysis in archaeological perspective' in M B Schiffer (ed) *Archaeological Method and Theory 4,* University of Arizona Press, Tucson and London.

Blackman, M J and Henrickson, R C, 1994: 'Ancient and modern clays and Phrygian pottery production at Gordion', *Amer J Archaeol,* 98.2, 338.

Blake, H and Davey, P, (eds) 1983: *Guidelines for the processing and publication of medieval pottery from excavations,* Dept of Environment Occasional Paper 5.

Blinkhorn, P, forthcoming: *Ipswich ware* MPRG Occasional Paper 2.

Bower, N W, Bromund, R H and Smith, R H, 1975: 'Atomic absorption for the archaeologist, an application to pottery from Pella of the Decapolis', *J Field Archaeol,* 2, 389–98.

Brooks, C and Mainman, A, 1984: 'Torksey ware viewed from the north' in Addyman P V and Black V E (eds) *Archaeological papers from York presented to MW Barley* York Archaeological Trust, 63–70.

Bruce-Mitford, R L S, 1964: 'A National Reference Collection of Medieval Pottery' *Medieval Archeol,* 8, 229–30.

Bucha, V, 1967: 'Intensity of the Earth's magnetic field during archaeological times in Czechoslovakia', *Archaeometry,* 10, 12–22.

Caley, E R, 1947: 'Results of a chemical examination of some specimens of Roman glaze from Tarsus', *Amer J Archaeol,* 51, 389–93.

Carr, C, 1993: 'Identifying individual vessels with X-radiography' *American Antiquity*, 58, 96–117.

Champion, S, 1995: 'Internet resources for archaeologists' in M Heyworth (ed) *British Archaeological Yearbook 1995–6,* CBA York, 250–60.

Charters, S, Evershed, R P and Denham, V, 1995: 'Evidence for the mixing of fats and waxes in archaeological ceramics ' *Archaeometry,* 37, 113–27.

Charters, S, Evershed, R P, Quye, A, Blinkhorn, P and Reeves, V, 1997: 'Simulation experiments for determining the use of ancient pottery vessels: the behaviour of epicuticular leaf wax during boiling of a leafy vegetable' *J Archaeol Sci,* 24.1, 1–7.

Chase, W T, 1971: 'Egyptian blue as a pigment and ceramic material', in Brill (ed), 1971, 80–90.

Cherry, J, 1986: 'The National Reference Collection of Medieval Pottery' *Medieval Ceramics,* 10, 125–30.

Clark, A J, 1993: 'Archaeomagnetic dating' in Clarke CP, Gardiner MF, Huggins PJ, *Excavations at Church St Waltham Abbey 1976–87: urban development and prehistoric evidence Essex Archaeol Hist,* 24, 111.

Clark, A J, Tarling, D H, and Noel, M, 1988: 'Developments in archaeomagnetic dating in Britain' *J Archaeol Sci,* 15, 645–67.

Clark, P A and Templar, R H, 1988: 'Thermoluminescent dating of materials which exhibit anomalous fading', *Archaeometry,* 31(1), 47–57.

Coleman-Smith, R and Pearson, T, 1988: *'Excavations in the Donyatt potteries'* Phillimore, Chichester.

Condamin, J, Formenti, F, Metais, M 0 and Blond, P, 1976: 'The application of gas MICHEL chromatography to the tracing of oil in ancient amphorae', *Archaeometry,* 18,195–201.

Council for British Archaeology (CBA), 1991: *Signposts for archaeological publication,* 3rd edn CBA.

CBA Archaeological Science Committee, 1990: 'Excavators and archaeological scientists', *British Archaeol News,* 5, 51–2 and 54.

Courty, M A and Roux, V, 1995: 'Identification of wheel-throwing on the basis of ceramic surface features and microfabrics', *J Archaeol Sci* 22, 17–50.

Cousins, D R and Dharmawardena, K, 1969: 'Use of Mössbauer spectroscopy in the study of ancient pottery', *Nature,* 223, 732–3.

Cowgill, G L, 1995: 'Unknown sampling bias is not a license to ignore statistical theory' in Anon (eds) *Methods in the Mountains Proc UISPP Commission IV conference in Australia 1994* 7–12.

Craig, O E and Collins, M J, 2000: 'An improved method for the immunological detection of mineral bound protein using hydrofluoric acid and direct capture', *J Immunol Methods* 236, 89–97.

Cranshaw, T E, Dale, B W and Longworth, G O, 1985: *Introduction to Mössbauer spectroscopy and its applications,* CUP.

Cumberpatch, C G, 1993: 'The circulation of Late La Tene slip decorated pottery in Slovakia, southern Poland and transdanubian Hungary', *Slovenskia archeolo'gia* 48 no 1, 59–81.

Dawson, D and Kent, O, 1999: 'Reduction fired low-temperature ceramics', *Post-Med Archaeol* 33, 164–178.

Day, R A, 1989: *How to write and publish a scientific paper.* (3rd edn) Cambridge University Press.

Delque Koliç E, 1995: 'Direct radiocarbon dating of pottery: selective heat treatment to retrieve smoke-derived carbon' *Radiocarbon* 37, 275–84.

Echallier, J C, 1991: 'Common and Pseudo-Ionian ware from le Pegue (Drôme) France: An analytical and archaeological problem' in Middleton and Freestone (eds) 1991, 63–70.

Eglington, T I, McNichol, A P, Benitez-Nelson, B C, Pearson, A, von Reden, K R, Schneider, R J, Bauer, J E and Druffel, E M, in press 'Gas chromatographic isolation of individual compounds from complex matrices for radiocarbon dating' *Analytical Chem.*

Eiland, M L and Williams, Q, 2000: 'Infra-red spectroscopy of ceramics from Tel Brak, Syria', *J Archaeol Sci* 27, 993–1006.

Eissa, N A, Sallam, H A, Saleh, S A, Taiel, F M and Kesthelyi L, 1974: 'Mössbauer effect study of ancient Egyptian pottery and the origin of the colour in Black Ware', in Bishay (ed) 1974, 85–98.

Evans, J, 1989: 'Neutron activation analysis and Romano-British pottery studies' in Henderson (ed) 1989, 136–62.

Evans, J, 1991: 'Organic traces and their contribution to the understanding of trade', *Studies in Mediterranean Archaeology* 90, 289–296.

Evershed, R P, Heron, C, Charters, S and Goad, L J, 1992: 'The survival of food residues: new methods of analysis, interpretation and application' *Proc British Acad,* 77, 187–208.

Feathers, J K, Berhane, M and May, L, 1998: 'Firing analysis of south-eastern Missouri Indian pottery using iron Mössbauer spectroscopy', *Archaeometry* 40.1, 59–70.

Fieller, N R J and Nicholson, P T, 1991: 'Grain size analysis of archaeological pottery: the use of statistical models' in Middleton and Freestone (eds) 1991, 71–110.

Fillieres, D, Harbottle, G and Sayre E V 1984: Neutron activation study of figurines, pottery, and workshop materials from the Athenian Agora, Greece, *J Field Archaeol,* 10, 55–69.

Fleming, S J, 1975: *Authenticity in Art The Scientific Detection of Forgery Institute of Physics.*

Fleming, S J and Swain, C P, 1992: 'Recent applications of PIXE spectrometry in archaeology II: characterisation of Chinese pottery exported to the Islamic world', *Nuclear Instruments and Methods in Physics Research* B64, 528–37.

Francaviglia, V, Minardi, M E and Palmieri, A, 1975: 'Comparative study of various samples of Etruscan bucchero by X-ray diffraction, X-ray spectrometry and Thermo-analysis', *Archae-ometry,* 17, 223–31

Freeman, I L and Rayment, D L, 1968: 'Scanning electron micrographs of some structural ceramic materials', *Trans Brit Ceram Soc,* 67, 611–8.

Freestone, I C, 1982: 'Applications and potential of electron probe micro-analysis in technological and provenance investigations of ancient ceramics' *Archaeometry,* 24, 99–116.

Freestone, I C, 1991: 'Extending Ceramic Petrology' in Middleton and Freestone (eds) 1991, 399–410.

Freestone, I C, 1995: 'Ceramic Petrography', *Amer J Archaeol* 99, 111–15.

Freestone, I C and Middleton, A P, 1987: 'Applications and potential of the analytical SEM in archaeology', *Mineralogical Magazine* 51, 21–31.

Freestone, I C, Middleton, A P and Meeks, N D, 1994: 'Significance of phosphate in ceramic bodies', *J Archaeol Sci,* 21.3, 425–6.

Freestone, I and Rigby, V, 1988: 'The introduction of Roman ceramic styles and techniques into Roman Britain: a case study from King Harry Lane cemetery, St Albans, Herts' in Sayre E V et al (eds) 1988, 109–115.

Fulford. M G, Huddleston, K, 1991: *The Current State of Romano-British Pottery Studies* English Heritage Occasional Paper, 1.

Gangas, N H J, Kostikas, A, Simopoulos, A and Vocotopoulou, J, 1971: 'Mossbauer spectroscopy of ancient Greek pottery', *Nature,* 229, 485–6.

Gerard, M, *et al.* 1997: 'The Manufacture of eulogies' in Maguire (ed) 1997, 9–24.

Gerard, M, Metzger, C, Person, A and Sodini, J-P, 1997: 'The manufacture of eulogies' in Maguire (ed), 9–24.

Gerrard, C, 1991: 'Sedimentary petrology and the archaeologist: the study of ancient ceramics' in Morton A C, Todd S P and Haughton, P D W (eds) *Developments in Sedimentary Proveance Studies Geolog Soc* Special Pub 57, 189–97.

Gillies, K J S and Urch, D S, 1983: 'Spectroscopic studies of iron and carbon in black-surfaced ware' *Archaeometry,* 25(1), 29–44.

Glover, 1990: 'Ban Don Ta Phet 1984–85' in Glover I C and Glover E (eds) *Southeast Asian Archaeology 1986* BAR International series 561, 139–83.

Grime, G W and Watt, F, 1993: 'A survey of recent PIXE applications in archaeometry and environmental sciences using the Oxford scanning proton microprobe facility' *Nuclear instruments & methods in physics research. Section B, Beam interactions with materials and atoms* B75, no 1–4, 495–503.

Gunnewag, J, Asarof Michelh, V and Perlman, I, 1994: 'Interregional contact between Tell en-Nasbeh and littoral Philistine centres in Canaan during Early Iron Age 1', *Archaeometry,* 36.2, 227–39.

Hatcher, H, Hedges, R E M, Pollard, A M and Kenrick, P M, 1980: 'Analysis of Hellenistic and Roman fine pottery from Benghazi', *Archaeometry,* 22(1), 133–45.

Hatcher, H, Tite, M S and Walsh, J N, 1995: 'A comparison of inductively-coupled plasma emission spectroscopy and Atomic absorption spectrophotometry analysis on standard reference silicate materials and ceramics', *Archaeometry,* 37(1), 83–94.

Hedges, R E M, Tiemei, C and Housley, R A, 1992: 'Results and methods in the radiocarbon dating of pottery' *Radiocarbon* 34.3, 906–15.

Henderson, J, (ed) 1989: *Scientific analysis in archaeology and its interpretation,* Oxford University Committee for Archaeol Mono 19/ Univ Calif Los Angeles Archaeol Research Tools 5.

Heron, C and Evershed, R P, 1993: 'The analysis of organic residues and the study of pottery use' in M B Schiffer (ed) *Archaeological Method and Theory 5,* University of Arizona Press, Tucson and London, 247–84.

Heron, C and Pollard, A M, 1987: 'The analysis of natural resinous materials from Roman amphorae' in E A Slater and J O Tate (eds) *Science and Archaeology, Glasgow 1987,* BAR British series 196, 1987, 29–47.

Hess, J and Perlman, I, 1974: 'Mossbauer spectra of iron in ceramics and their relation to pottery colours', *Archaeometry,* 16, 137–152.

Higgins, T, 1997: 'An introduction to digital image processing' in Lang and Middleton 1997, 167–82.

Hofmann, U, 1962: 'The chemical basis of ancient Greek vase painting', *Angewandte Chemie 1,* 341–50.

Howard, H and Morris, E, 1981: *Production and distribution: a ceramic viewpoint,* BAR International series 120.

Hudson, J, 1989: 'The York Medieval Tile-making Experiment – A Potter's Tale', *Medieval Ceramics,* 13, 43–52.

Hughes, M J, 1995: 'Application of scientific analytical methods to Spanish medieval ceramics' in C Gerrard, A Gutierrez and A G Vince (eds) *Spanish medieval ceramics in Spain and the British Isles* BAR International Series 610, Oxford, 359–66.

Hughes, M J, Cowell, M R and Craddock, P T, 1976: 'Atomic absorption techniques in archaeology, *Archaeometry,* 18, 19–37.

Hughes, M J, Cherry, J, Freestone I C and Leese, M, 199X: 'Neutron activation analysis and petrology of Medieval English decorated floor tiles from the Midlands' in I C Freestone, C Johns and T Potter (eds) *Current Research in Ceramics: Thin Section Studies,* British Museum Occasional Paper 32.

Hughes, M J, Cowell, M R and Hook, D R, (eds) 1991: 'Neutron Activation and Plasma Emission Spectrometry Analysis in Archaeology', *British Museum Occasional Paper* 82, British Museum.

Hunter, R W, 1979: 'St Neots Type Ware' Appendix to M R McCarthy, 'The Pottery' in J H Williams, *St Peter's Street, Northampton: Excavations 1973–76,* 230–40.

Hurst, D and Freestone, I C, 1996: 'Lead Glazing Technique from a Medieval Kiln Site at Hanley Swan, Worcestershire' *Medieval Ceramics,* 20, 13–18.

Insitute of Field Arcaeologists (IFA), 1991: *Guidelines for Finds Work*, IFA Finds Group.

IFA, 1998: *Report of the convenor of the working agreements working party.*

Isphording, W C, 1974: 'Combined thermal and X-ray diffraction technique for identification of ceramic-ware temper and paste materials', *American Antiquity,* 39, 477–83.

Jacobson, L, Pineda, C A, Morris, D and Peisach, M, 1994: 'PIXE analysis of pottery from the northern Cape Province of South Africa' *Nuclear instruments & methods in physics research. Section B, Beam interactions with materials and atoms* B75, no 1–4, 901–3.

Jarvis, K E, Gray, A L and Houk, R S, 1992: *A handbook of Inductively-coupled plasma mass spectrometry* Blackie.

Johannson, S A E and Campbell, J L, 1988: *PIXE: a novel technique for elemental analysis*, Chichester.

Johnson, J S, Clark, J, Miller-Antonio, S, Robins, D, Schiffer, M B and Skibo, J M, 1988: 'Effects of Firing Temperatures on the Fate of Naturally Occurring Organic Matter in Clays', *J Archaeol Sci,* 15.4, 403–414.

Jones, D, 1997: 'Analysis of lime deposits' in A G Johnston, P J Foster and B Bellamy 'The excavation of two late medieval kilns with associated buildings at Glapthorn, near Oundle, Northants.' *Medieval Ceramics* 21, 3–42.

Jones, J G, 1993: 'Analysis of pollen and phytoliths in residue from a Colonial period ceramic vessel' in D M Pearsall and D R Piperno (eds), *Current research in phytolith analysis: applications in archaeology and paleoecology* MASCA research papers in science and archaeology 10 ch 5.

Jones, R E, 1986: *Greek and Cypriot pottery: a review of scientific studies.* Fitch Laboratory Occasional Paper 1 British School of Archaeology, Athens.

Keirs, C D and Vickers, T J, 1977: 'D C plasma arcs for elemental analysis' *Applied Spectroscopy,* 31 (4), 273–283.

Kilikoglou, V, Maniatis, Y and Grimanos, A P, 1988: 'The effect of purification and firing of clays on trace element provenance studies', *Archaeometry* 30, 37–46.

Kingery, W D, 1974: 'A technological characterization of two Cypriot ceramics' in Bishay 1974, 169–86.

Kingery, W D, (ed) 1993: *The social and cultural context of new ceramic technologies* Ceramics and Civilization 6 American Ceramic Society Westerville, Ohio.

Kingery, W D and Vandiver, P B, 1986: *Ceramic masterpieces,* New York.

Koh Choo, C K, 1995: 'A Scientific Study of Traditional Korean Celadons and their modern developments' *Archaeometry,* 37(1), 53–81.

La Niece, S, 1997: 'Restoration, pastiche and fakes' in Lang and Middleton, 1997, 155–66.

Lambert, J B, Xue, L, Weydert, J M and Winter, J H, 1990: 'Oxidation states of iron in Bahamian pottery by X-ray photoelectron spectroscopy', *Archaeometry,* 32(1), 47–54.

Lang, J and Middleton, A, 1997: *Radiography of Cultural Materials*, Butterworth.

Lima-De-Faria, A, 1995: 'The Genetic Information Preserved in Ceramics – A New Tool for Archaeological Studies' *Medieval Ceramics,* 19, 99–100.

London, G, 1981: 'Dung-tempered clay', *J Field Archaeol* 8, 189–95.

MacDonald, A, 1988: 'An attempt to make a replica C14th Lincoln ware jug', *Medieval Ceramics,* 12, 23–31.

MacKenzie, K D and Cardile, D M, 1990: 'A ^{57}Fe Mössbauer study of black coring phenomena in clay-based ceramic materials', *J Mater Sci* 25, 2937–42.

Maguire, H, (ed) 1997: *Materials analysis of Byzantine pottery* Dumbarton Oaks, Washington.

Mainman, A, 1982: 'Studies of Anglo-saxon pottery in Canterbury' in I Freestone, C Johns and T Potter (eds) *Current Research in ceramics* British Museum Occ Pap 32, 93–100.

Makundi, I N, Waern-Sperber, A and Ericsson, I, 1989: 'A Mossbauer study of the black colour in Early Cypriote and Nubian C-group black-topped pottery', *Archaeometry,* 31(1), 54–65.

Maniatis, Y, Jones, R E, Whitbread, I K, Kostikas, A, Simopoulos, A, Karakolos, C and William, C K, 1984: 'Punic amphoras found at Corinth, Greece: an investigation of their origin and technology *J Field Archaeol,* 11, 205–22.

Maniatis,Y and Tite, M S, 1981: 'Technological examination of Neolithic-Bronze age pottery from central and south-east Europe and from the Near East' *J Archaeol Sci,* 8, 59–76.

Manning, P G, 1975: 'On the origin of grey and black "colours" of ancient pottery: role of Fe and Ti4+ ions', *Archaeometry,* 17, 233–235.

MAP 2, 1991: *Management of Archaeological Projects*, 2nd edn English Heritage.

Mason, R B and Tite, M S, 1994: 'The beginnings of Islamic stonepaste technology', *Archaeometry,* 36.1, 77–91.

Medieval Pottery Research Group, forthcoming: 'Minimum standards for the processing, recording, analysis and publication of post-roman ceramics' MPRG Occasional Paper.

Mellor, M, 1994: Medieval Ceramic Studies in England: A review for English Heritage, Norwich.

Middleton, A P, 1987: 'Technological investigation of the coatings on some haematite-coated pottery from southern England' *Archaeometry,* 29, 250–61

Middleton, A P, 1995: 'Integrated approaches to the understanding of early ceramics: the role of radiography', in B Fabbri (ed) *The Cultural Ceramic Heritage, Fourth Euro Ceramics,* 14, 63–74.

Middleton, A P, Freestone, I C and Leese, M N, 1985: 'Textural analysis of ceramic thin sections: evaluation of grain sampling procedures', *Archaeometry,* 27, 64–74.

Middleton, A P and Freestone, I C, (eds) 1991: *Recent Developments in Ceramic Petrology,* British Museum Occasional Paper 81.

Mirti, P, 1998: 'On the use of colour co-ordinates to evaluate firing temperatures of ancient pottery' *Archaeometry,* 40.1, 45–57.

Mirti, P, Casoli, A, Barra Bagnasco, M and Preacco Ancona, M C, 1995: 'Fine Ware from Locri Epizephin: A Provenance Study by Inductively Coupled Plasma Emission Spectroscopy' *Archaeometry,* 37(1), 41–51.

Mommsen, H, Beier, T, Heimermenn, D, Hein, A, Ittameier, D and Podzuweit, C H, 1994: 'Neutron activation analysis of selected sherds from Prophitis Ilias (Argolid, Greece): a closed Late Helladic II settlement complex' *J Archaeol Sci,* 21.2, 163–71.

Moorhouse, S, 1986: 'Non-dating Uses of Medieval Pottery', *Medieval Ceramics,* 10, 85–123.

Morris, E and Woodward, A, ( ) 'Ceramic Petrology and Prehistoric Pottery Studies' *Proc Prehist Soc.*

Munsell Color, 1975: *Munsell Soil Color Charts,* Macbeth Division of Kollmorgen Corporation, Baltimore.

Murphy, P, 1985: 'The cereals and crop weeds' in S West (ed) 'West Stow the Anglo-Saxon village' 1, *East Anglian Archaeol*, 24, 100–108.

Musty, J W G, 1974: 'Medieval pottery kilns', in V Evison, H Hodges, J G Hurst (eds) *Medieval Pottery From Excavations: Studies presented to Gerald Clough Dunning*, Baker, 41–65.

Neff, H, (ed) 1992: *Chemical Characterisation of Ceramic Pastes in Archaeology* Monographs in World Archaeology 7, Prehistory Press, Madison.

Neff, H, Bishop, R L and Arnold, D E 1988: 'Reconstructing ceramic production from ceramic compositional data; an example from Guatemala' *J Field Archaeol*, 15 339–48.

Nenk, B and Walker, H, 1991: 'An aquamanile and a spouted jug in Lyveden-Stanion Ware' *Medieval Ceramics*, 15 25–8.

Newell, R W, 1995: 'Some notes on 'splashed glazes'' *Medieval Ceramics*, 19, 77–88.

Newman, M E, Ceri, H and Kooyman, B, 1996: 'The use of immunological techniques in the analysis of archaeological materials – a response to Eisele' *Antiquity*, 70, 677–82.

Orton, C R, 1980: *Mathematics in Archaeology*, Collins.

Orton, C R, 1998–9 'Minimum standards in statistics and sampling', *Medieval Ceramics* 22–3, 135–8.

Orton, C R, 2000: *Sampling in Archaeology*, Cambridge University Press.

Orton, C R, 2001: 'Reinventing the sherd: 25 years of pottery statistics', *Medieval Ceramics* 24.

Orton, C, Tyers, P and Vince, A, 1993: *Pottery in Archaeology*, Cambridge University Press.

Owen, J V and Day, T E, 1994: 'Estimation of the bulk composition of fine-grained media from microchemical and backscatter-image analysis: application to biscuit wasters from the Bow Factory site, London' *Archaeometry*, 36.2, 217–26.

PCRG 1997: *Guidelines for the Analysis of Later Prehistoric Pottery* PCRG Occasional Paper 2.

Peacock, D P S, 1967: 'The heavy mineral analysis of pottery; a preliminary report' *Archaeometry*, 10, 97–100.

Peacock, D P S, 1968: 'A petrological study of certain Iron Age pottery from western England', *Proc Prehist Soc*, 34, 414–427.

Peacock, D P S, 1973: 'The black-burnished pottery industry in Dorset', in *Current Research in Romano-British Coarse Pottery*, ed Detsicas A, Council British Archaeol Res Rep 10, 63–65.

Peacock, D P S, 1977a: 'Pompeian Redware' in Peacock (ed) 1977, 147–62.

Peacock, D P S, 1977b: 'Ceramics in Roman and medieval archaeology', in Peacock (ed) 1977, 21–33.

Peacock, D P S, (ed) 1977: *Pottery and early commerce. Characterisation and trade* in *Roman and later ceramics*.

Peacock, D P S and Thomas, A C, 1967: 'Class "E" imported post-Roman pottery: a suggested origin', *Cornish Archaeol*, 6, 35–46.

Peacock, D P S and Williams, D, 1986: *Amphorae and the Roman economy*, Longman.

Perinet, G, 1960: 'Contribution de la diffraction des rayons X a l'evaluation de la temperature de cuisson d'une ceramique', *Trans 7th International Ceramic Congress, 371–6.*

Philpotts, A R and Wilson, N, 1994: 'Application of petrofabric and phase equilibria analysis to the study of a potsherd', *J Archaeol Sci,* 21.5, 607–18.

Picon, M, Carre, C, Cordoliana, M L, Vichy, M and Mignard, J L, 1975: 'Composition of the La Hernandez, J A, Graufesenque, Banassac and Montans terra sigillata, *Archaeometry, 17,* 191–9.

Picon, M, Vichy, M and Meille, E, 1971: 'Composition of the Lezoux, Lyon and Arezzo Samian ware', *Archaeometry,* 13, 191–208.

Pollard, A M, 1995: 'Why teach Heisenberg to archaeologists?', *Antiquity* 69, 242–7.

Pollard, A M and Hatcher, H, 1994: 'Oriental ceramic body compositions 1: north China', *Archaeometry,* 36(1), 41–62.

Post medieval Archaeology, 1968: 'National Reference Collection for Post-medieval Ceramics' *Post Med Arch* 2, 217.

Qin G, Pan X and Li S, 1989: 'A firing study of terracotta warriors and horses of the Qin dynasty (221 BC)', *Archaeometry,* 31(1), 3–12.

Ramola, J A, Larrechi, M S and Rius, F X, 1993: 'Chemometric characterization of 5th century AD amphora-producing centers in the Mediterranean', *Talanta,* 40.11, 1749–57.

Redknap, M, 1988: 'The National Reference Collection for Medieval and Later Pottery for Wales' *Medieval and Later Pottery in Wales,* 10, 33–39.

Rehman, F, Robinson, V J, Newton, G W A and Shennans, S J, 1991: 'Neutron activation and the Bell Beaker folk' in Budd P, Chapman B, Jackson C, Janaway R and Ottaway B (eds) *Archaeological Science 1989: proceedings of a conference on the application of scientific technology to archaeology, Bradford September 1989.* Oxbow Monograph 9, 95–103.

Reinders, J, Hambach, U, Krumsiek, K, Sanke, M and Strack, N, 1999: 'An archaeomagnetic study of pottery kilns from Bruhl-Pingsdorf (Germany)' *Archaeometry,* 41.2, 413–20.

Rice, P M, 1987: *Pottery analysis: a sourcebook*, Chicago.

Rigby, V, Middleton, A P and Freestone, I C, 1989: 'The Prunay workshop: technological examination of La Tene bichrome painted pottery from Champagne', *World Archaeol,* 21, 1–16.

Rudling, D, 1984–5: 'A Roman tilery at Hartfield, East Sussex', *Bull Experimental Firing Group,* 3, 25–33.

Rye, 0 S, 1976: 'Keeping your temper under control: materials and the manufacture of Papuan pottery', *Archaeology and Physical Anthropology in Oceania,* 11, 106–37.

Rye, 0 S, 1977: 'Pottery manufacturing techniques: X-ray studies', *Archaeometry,* 19, 205–10.

Rye, O S and Duerden, P, 1982: 'Papuan pottery sourcing by PIXE: preliminary studies', *Archaeometry* 24, 59–64.

Sayre, E V and Who, (eds) 1988: *Materials issues in art and archaeology: symposium held April 6–8 1988 Reno, Nevada, USA.* Materials Research Society, 25–32.

Schmitt, A, 1998: 'Amphorae from Lyons: petrographic and chemical arguments', *Archaeometry* 40.2, 293–310.

Shennan, S, 1997: *Quantifying Archaeology* (2nd edn) Edinburgh University Press.

Shepard, A 0, 1942: *Rio Grande glaze paint ware, a study illustrating the place of ceramic technological analysis in archaeological research,* Publ 528, Camegie Institution of Washington.

Shepard, A O, 1966: 'Rio Grande glaze paint pottery: a test of petrographic analysis', in F R Matson (ed) *Ceramics and Man*, 62–87, Methuen.

Shepard, A O, 1971: 'Ceramic analysis: the interrelations of methods; the relations of analysts and archaeologists', in Brill (ed) 1971, 55–64.

Shepard, A O, 1976: *Ceramics for the Archaeologist*, Publ 609, Carnegie Institution of Washington (8th Printing).

Shepherd, L A, 1997: 'Optical dating of archaeological ceramics' in A Sinclair, E Slater and J Gowlett (eds) *Archaeological Sciences 1995*, Oxbow mono. 64, 163-9.

Sheridan, A, 1989: 'Pottery production in Neolithic Ireland: a petrological and chemical study', in Henderson (ed) 1989, 112–35.

Sherriff, B L, Tisdale, M A, Sayer, B G, Schwarz, H P and Kniff, M, 1995: 'Nuclear magnetic resonance, spectroscopic and isotopic analysis of carbonized residues from sub-arctic Canadian prehistoric pottery', *Archaeometry*, 37(1), 95–111.

Shoval, S, 1993: 'The burning temperature of a Persian period pottery kiln at Tel Michal, Israel, estimated from the composition of slag-like material formed in its wall', *J Thermal Anal*, 39 no 8–9, 1157–68.

Shoval, S, Beck, P, Kirsh, Y, Levy, D, Gaft, M and Yadin, E, 1991: 'Rehydroxylation of clay minerals and hydration in ancient pottery from the "Land of Geshur"' *J Thermal Anal*, 37.7 1579–92.

Shoval, S, Gaft, M, Beck, P and Kirsh, Y, 1993: 'Thermal behaviour of limestone and monocrystalline caclite tempers during firing and their use in ancient vessels' *J thermal anal*, 40.1 263–73.

Sillar, B and Tite, M S, 2000: 'The challenge of 'technological choices' for material science approaches in archaeology', *Archaeometry* 42, 2–20.

Stemler, A, 1990: 'Scanning electron microscopic analysis of plant impressions in pottery from the sites of Kaderoe, EL Zakiab, Um Direiwa and El-Kadada' *Archeologie du Nil Moyen*, 4, 87–105.

Steponaitis, V P, 1984: 'Technological studies of prehistoric pottery from Alabama: physical properties and vessel function' in S E Van der Leeuw and A C Pritchard (eds) *The Many Dimensions of Pottery* University of Amsterdam, 219–228.

Stilke, H, Hein, A and Mommsen, H, 1996: 'Results of Neutron Activation Analysis on Tating Ware and the Mayen Industry' *Medieval Ceramics*, 20, 25–32.

Storey, J M V, Symonds, R P, Hart, F A, Smith, D M and Walsh, J N, 1989: 'A chemical investigation of 'Colchester' samian by means of ICP-AES', *J Roman Pottery Stud* 2, 33–43.

Stos-Fertner, Z, Hedges, R E M and Evely, R D G, 1979: 'The application of the XRF-XRD method to the analysis of the pigments of Minoan painted pottery', *Archaeometry*, 21, 187–194.

Streeten, A, 1980: 'Potters, kilns and markets in medieval Sussex: a preliminary study' *Sussex Arch Colln* 118, 105–118.

Study Group for Roman Pottery (SGRP), 1994: *Guidelines for the archiving of Roman pottery*, Guidelines advisory document 1.

Swan, V G, 1984: *The pottery kilns of Roman Britain* RCHM Supplementary Series 5.

Tarling, D H, 1983: *Palaeomagnetism*, London.

Tarling, D H, 1991: 'Archaeomagnetism and palaeo-magnetism II. Magnetic dating and other applications' *Euro courses: advanced scientific techniques,* 1.1, 237–50.

Taylor, R E and Aitken, M J, 1997: *Chronometric dating in archaeology* Advances in archaeological and museum science 2, Plenum.

Tite, M S, 1972: *Methods of Physical Examination in Archaeology,* Seminar Press, London and New York.

Tite, M S, 1988: 'The study of ancient ceramic technologies: past achievements and future prospects' in *Science and Archaeology Glagow 1987* E A Slater and J O Tate (eds), BAR British series 196 (i) 9–19.

Tite, M S, 1989: 'Iznik pottery: an investigation of the microstructures associated with the different methods of glazing' *Archaeometry,* 28, 115–32.

Tite, M S, 1992: 'The Impact of Electron Microscopy on Ceramic Studies' in A M Pollard (ed) *New Developments in Archaeological Science,* Proc British Academy, 77,111–131.

Tite, M S and Bimson, M, 1991: 'A technological study of English porcelain' *Archaeometry,* 33(1), 3–27.

Tite, M S, Hughes, M J, Freestone, I C, Meeks, N D and Bimson, M, 1990: 'Technological characterisation of refractory ceramics from Timna' in B Rothenberg (ed) *The Ancient Metallurgy of copper: archaeology-experiment-theory,* 158–75.

Tite, M S and Maniatis, Y, 1975: 'Examination of ancient pottery using the scanning electron microscope', *Nature* 257, 122–3. (Also in *Trans Brit Ceram Soc,* 74,19–22).

Tomber, R and Dore, J, 1998: *The National Roman Fabric Reference Collection – A Handbook* MOLAS monograph 2.

Topping, P G and MacKenzie, A B, 1988: 'A test for the use of Neutron activation analysis for clay source characterisation' *Archaeometry,* 30(1), 92–101.

Tubb, A, Parker, A J and Nickless, G, 1980: 'The analysis of Romano-British pottery by atomic absorption spectrophotometry' *Archaeometry,* 22, 153–171.

Turrell, G and Corset, J, 1996: *Raman Microscopy: Developments and Applications* Academic Press

van der Leeuw, S E, 1994: 'Cognitive aspects of technique' in C Renfrew and E Zubrow (eds) *The ancient mind Elements of cognitive archaeology,* Cambridge University Press 135–42.

van der Veen, M, 1993: 'Grain impressions in early Anglo-saxon pottery from Mucking' in H Hamerow, *Excavations at Mucking* vol 2, *The Anglo-saxon settlement*, English Heritage archaeol rep 21, 80–81.

Vandiver, P B, 1988: 'The implications of variations in ceramic technology: the forming of Neolithic storage vessels in China and the Near East' *Archaeomaterials,* 2, 139–74.

Vince, A G, 1981: 'The use of petrology in the study of medieval ceramics: case studies from southern England' *Medieval Ceramics* 8, 31–45.

Vince, A G, 1989: 'The petrography of Saxon and early medieval pottery in the Thames Valley' in J Henderson (ed) 1989 163–77.

Vince, A G (ed), forthcoming: 'The United Kingdom ceramic thin-section database', *Internet Archaeol* (http://intarch.ac.uk)

Vogt, C, Bouquillon, A, Dubus, M and Querré, G, 1997: 'Glazed wall tiles of Constantinople' in Maguire (ed) 1997, 51–65.

Waksman, S Y and Spicer, J-M, 1997: 'Byzantine ceramics excavated in Pergamon' in Maguire (ed) 1997, 105–118.

Wallis, F S and Evens, E D, 1934: 'Report on the heavy minerals contained in the coarse Pant-y-Saer pottery', *Archaeol Cambrensis,* 89, 29–32.

Wardle, P, 1992: *Earlier Prehistoric pottery production and ceramic petrology in Britain.* BAR British series 225 (iii).

Watson, F J, 1985: 'Romano-British kiln building and firing a replica', *Pottery Quart* 5, 72–5.

Whitbread, I K, 1991: 'Image and data processing in ceramic petrology' in Middleton and Freestone (eds) 1991.

Widemann, F, Picon, M, Asaro, F, Michel, H V and Perlman, I, 1975: 'A Lyons branch of the pottery-making firm of Ateius of Arezzo', *Archaeometry,* 17, 45–9.

Williams, D F, 1977: 'The Romano-British black burnished industry: An essay on characterization by heavy mineral analysis' in Peacock 1977b.

Williams, D F, 1983: 'Petrology of Ceramics' in *The Petrology of Archaeological Artifacts* (ed) D R C Kempe and A C Harvey, Oxford. 301–29.

Williams, D F, 1994: 'A thin section examination of Middle Saxon Ipswich ware pottery', in P Blinkhorn, forthcoming.

Williams, J, Li, W, Jenkins, D A and Livens, R G, 1974: 'An analytical study of the composition of Roman coarse ware from the fort of Bryn y Gefeiliau (Caer Llugwy) in Snowdonia', *J Archaeol Sci,* 1, 47–67.

Woods, A J, 1986: 'Form, fabric and function: some observations on the cooking pot in antiquity' in W D Kingery (ed) *Ceramics and civilization II: Technology and style,* American Ceramics Society, Westerville, Ohio, 157–72.

Woods, A J, 1989: 'Fired with enthusiasm: experimental open firings at Leicester University' in A Gibson (ed) *Midlands prehistory: some recent and current researches into the prehistory of Central England* BAR British series 294, 196–226.

Young, C J, (ed) 1980: 'Guidelines for the processing and publication of Roman pottery from excavations', *Dir Anc Monuments Hist Build, Occasional Paper Series* 4, Department of the Environment, London.

Zimmerman, D W and Huxtable, J, 1969: 'Recent applications and developments in thermo-luminescent dating', *Archaeometry,* 1 1, 105–8.

Index:
Analytical techniques and their acronyms